Celebration Days
Holidays for Dull Days

By
Marilee Whiting Woodfield

Cover illustration by
Julie Anderson

Inside illustrations by
Marilee Whiting Woodfield

Publisher
Instructional Fair · TS Denison
Grand Rapids, Michigan

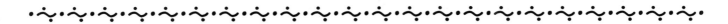

Instructional Fair · TS Denison

Dedication

To Ginger, who saw the potential and made it all possible; Craig, who had the determination and encouragement to see me through; and Kira, Tyler, and Daniel, my all-time favorite preschoolers who have taught me that truly any day can be a celebration.

Credits

Author: Marilee Whiting Woodfield
Cover Illustration: Julie Anderson
Inside Illustrations: Marilee Whiting Woodfield
Project Director: Debra Olson Pressnall
Editors: Debra Olson Pressnall & Karen Seberg
Cover Art Direction: Darcy Bell-Myers
Graphic Layout: Deborah Hanson McNiff

About the Author

Marilee Woodfield, who once swore she would never set foot in hot and "buggy" Texas again, currently resides in Carrollton, Texas, with her husband and four children (and loves Texas after all—in spite of the heat and bugs). When not teaching preschool or driving the family taxi service, Marilee enjoys spending time with her family, bargain shopping, and dabbling in home improvement projects—or anything else that involves creating a terrific mess.

Although she has learned that great ideas can emerge from just about anywhere, Marilee especially enjoys the inspiration gained from her experience and association with many children and teachers as a preschool educator and director. Marilee began her professional career by studying Early Childhood Education at Utah State and Brigham Young Universities, graduating with a degree in Human Development. Marilee claims that her short attention span is the result of 13 years of preschool and that pure torture in having to sit still and do nothing. As a result, many ideas for celebration activities are now offered in this book.

Standard Book Number 1-56822-529-6
Holidays for Dull Days
Copyright © 1999 by Ideal • Instructional Fair Publishing Group
a division of Tribune Education
2400 Turner Avenue NW
Grand Rapids, Michigan 49544

Table of Contents

To the Teacher

It is past the new year and there is little to look forward to until the weather breaks, or you have survived the heat of summer, but it will be weeks until it starts to feel like autumn. Perhaps you are tired of the "HYPE" associated with celebrating the "traditional" holidays—*Holidays for Dull Days* is just the cure for the holiday blues. No need to wait for a traditional holiday for fun—create your own classroom traditions by celebrating "Pig Day," "National Mosquito Awareness Weekend," "Me Week," "Bathtub Party Day," and many others.

Holidays for Dull Days is a compilation of cross-curricular learning activities based on little known holidays and celebrations—many that are recognized in the United States as official "National Days." The activities focus on a variety of developmental skills that disguise learning as fun.

Using readily available materials and reproducible patterns for headbands, game cards, and other game pieces, your theme celebration can be ready in just minutes. Many of the activities use food products as teaching tools. It is suggested that any of the food products that you use be handled in such a way so that the projects can be eaten. Wherever possible, suggestions for alternative supplies have been recommended. Of course, any of the activities should be adapted according to your discretion so that the celebration is a rewarding and age-appropriate experience for all children in your classroom.

As you celebrate, there will be many opportunities to inspire the children to look at everyday themes in extraordinary ways. You may wish to take this opportunity to encourage the children to explore more through further research by thinking of questions to investigate, "reading" books on related topics, and "recording" their thoughts in journals.

Regardless of your reason for hosting a theme celebration, you will love incorporating *Holidays for Dull Days* into your curriculum as it will make any day a special day.

Oatmeal Month

Oatmeal is best known for great breakfasts, but did you know that the carbohydrates in oatmeal can give you a great energy boost any time of the day?

Use this unit as a springboard for discussion and exploration of the importance of eating a healthful breakfast every day! Talk about the varieties of "breakfast" foods available and how fruits and dairy products can round out the children's nutritional needs for a great start each day.

Oatmeal Shakers

Fill a small paper cup one-third full of dry oats. Seal the top of the cup by covering it with plastic wrap or waxed paper and securing it with a rubber band. Shake your oatmeal shaker while listening to a music tape, or make your own rhythm band.

Quick Oats/Slow Oats

How much quicker are quick-cooking oats? Cook a small amount of oatmeal using regular slow-cooking oats and another using quick oats as directed on the cartons. Do quick oats and slow oats taste differently from one another? Use comparing and contrasting skills to decide which kind really is best!

Oatmeal Sandbox

Place a large amount of dry oatmeal in a large bowl or tub. Provide measuring cups, spoons, and other small containers to sift, pour, and measure.

Variations: Place a sheet of dark paper on the bottom of a square pan or box lid. Fill the pan with oatmeal so that the paper is covered with dry oatmeal flakes. Have the children practice writing numbers, letters, spelling words, or names in the oatmeal with their fingers. Simply shake the box to "erase" the work for more practice.

Make several copies of the oatmeal cookie shape (see page 7). Create a set of flashcards (e.g., spelling words, letters, math facts) on index cards. Working with partners, have the children take turns; one child gives the questions and the other writes the answers in the oatmeal box. Using a three-minute timer, see how many questions the second child can answer correctly. An oatmeal cookie shape is earned for every correct answer. When finished, five cookie shapes can be traded in for a sticker or other reward, if desired.

Granola

Have the children help you measure and mix the following ingredients to make some yummy granola. (Be sure to send everyone home with a sample).

Combine:
2½ c. (592 ml) oats
1 c. (237 ml) coconut
½ c. (118 ml) almonds, chopped
½ c. (118 ml) sunflower seeds
½ c. (118 ml) wheat germ
Combine, then add to oat mixture:
½ c. (120 ml) honey
¼ c. (60 ml) cooking oil

Spread in a 9" x 13" (23 x 33 cm) pan and bake at 300° for 45–50 minutes, stirring every 15 minutes. Add ½ c. (118 ml) dried fruit and ½ c. (118 ml) raisins if desired. Continue stirring every 15 minutes as the mixture cools.

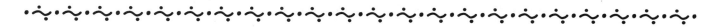

Oatmeal Cookie Color Game

Make two copies of the Oatmeal Cookie Color Cards on heavy cardstock. Color each card the color indicated. Cut out each card and laminate if desired.

Put each ingredient listed in the recipe below into a clear, resealable plastic bag (you may either premeasure the ingredients, or have the children help you measure each food item as you add it to your batter.) Gather all utensils and equipment necessary to mix the cookies. Tape one of the color cards onto the outside of each ingredient bag. Hide the bags around the room. Cut apart the second set of color cards and place them in a brown paper bag.

To play: Have the children take turns drawing color cards from the brown paper bag. Ask the child to identify the color and then search the room for the matching color card and cookie ingredient. Add the ingredient to a large bowl and repeat until all the ingredients have been added to the cookie mixture. Prepare the batter. Bake the cookies as directed and enjoy your results!

Oatmeal Cookies

Mix until creamy:
    ¾ c. (177 ml) shortening
    1½ c. (355 ml) brown sugar
    2 eggs
Add and mix together:
    ¼ c. (60 ml) milk
    ½ tsp. (2.5 ml) cloves
    1 tsp. (5 ml) salt
    ½ tsp. (2.5 ml) cinnamon
    2 c. (474 ml) flour
    ¾ tsp. (3.75 ml) soda
    1½ c. (355 ml) oats
Place spoonfuls of cookie mixture on the baking sheets. Bake at 325° for 10–15 minutes.

Oatmeal Box Figures

Request parent donations of empty oatmeal canisters several weeks before hosting this celebration day. Prepare the oatmeal boxes by covering them with white construction paper. Invite the children to turn the oatmeal boxes into creative figures by using paint, construction paper, yarn, and other craft odds and ends to decorate them.

Variation: Fill several oatmeal canisters with varying amounts of rolled oats. Seal the containers to prevent spills. Have the children use the canisters to balance and weigh objects in the classroom or compare the weight of a canister to their own weights (such as, "It takes 25 of this canister to equal what I weigh"). They can also arrange the canisters in order from heaviest to lightest based on shaking and estimating each canister's weight. Record the results.

Oatmeal Sampling

To enjoy this activity, prepare a batch of unflavored cooked oatmeal and provide spoons, several small sample-sized cups, and a variety of toppings and spices such as cinnamon, sugar, brown sugar, nuts, fresh fruit, jams, raisins, flavored syrups, etc. Let each child make his/her own oatmeal concoction by selecting any of the toppings (or more than one, if desired) to create unique oatmeal dishes.

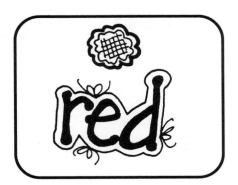

Happy Un-Birthday Party

*Children in some countries such as China
celebrate their birthdays at the beginning of the year.
Start this year out with a bang by celebrating every child's un-birthday.*

Birthday in a Bag

Fill a large paper bag with an assortment of birthday decorations, such as balloons, paper streamers, party hats, banners, and noisemakers. Have the children guess what is inside the bag. After each child has had the opportunity to make a suggestion, open the bag and reveal its contents. Tell the children they will be celebrating their un-birthdays today and singing "Happy Un-Birthday to Me!" Have the children help you decorate the room using the contents of the bag.

Variation: Divide the class into small groups. Have the groups plan a party by making a planning list (or dictating their ideas to an adult) of things they would need to host a birthday party.

Variation: A few days before doing this activity, send home a parent note requesting that each child bring an inexpensive wrapped gift to give away in an un-birthday gift exchange. (It is helpful to specify a dollar amount such as "less than $2." Have a couple of extra small gifts on hand in case a child forgets, so that all the children may participate).

Un-Birthday Cupcakes

Prepare cake batter using a boxed cake mix and following the directions on the package. Place empty ice cream cone cups in muffin tins and fill them two-thirds full with cake batter. Bake as directed for cupcakes.
Cool, then decorate the cupcakes using frosting and cake-decorating candies. For the party, add a birthday candle to each and light them as everyone makes a wish and sings "Happy Un-Birthday to Me" one more time.

Card/Gift Exchange

Using markers and a piece of construction paper folded in half, have each child decorate an un-birthday card for another child. Place the un-birthday cards in a big box, shake, and let each child choose a card from the box as his/her very own un-birthday card.

Balloon Pop

Write down a list of tasks on small slips of paper, one for each child, such as: "Touch your toes 10 times," "Count backwards from 10," "Sing 'Twinkle, Twinkle Little Star'." Slip a folded task suggestion inside each balloon, then inflate the balloons. Store the balloons in a large box or garbage bag. Let the children take turns popping a balloon to reveal the suggested task. Have all the children perform the task each time. Repeat until all the balloons have been popped.

Variation: To make the activity more challenging for the students, write on the slips of paper simple math equations, logic problems, skill development such as counting backwards from 100 by 10s, or review questions about a recent unit of study.

Balloon Bop

Inflate enough balloons so that there is one for each child. Let each child select a balloon and label it with his/her name using a permanent marker. Turn on some music and encourage the children to bop their balloons in the air to the beat of the music. Suggested movements: Try bopping with your other hand, behind your back, with your head, while spinning or marching in circles, or bop back and forth with a friend.

Stick the Nose on the Clown

Enlarge and copy the clown pattern on page 10. Color it as desired and laminate it for durability. Cut red construction paper circles, one for each child. Attach a rolled piece of masking tape to the back of each circle. Ready to take aim? Have the children take turns trying to stick the nose on the clown in the correct place while blindfolded.

Counting Candles

Make a copy of Counting Candles on page 11 for each child. Cut several strips of construction paper ½" x 3" (13 x 75 mm) in various colors. Have the children each color a cake and glue as many "candles" (construction paper strips) onto the cake as desired. Count the number of candles on the cake and write the number on the top of the page.

Variations: Have the children add together all the candles of the other children sitting at their table, the total number of candles in the classroom, of the boys, of the girls, etc. Have the children guess or estimate how many candles would be on the teacher's cake, librarian's,

principal's, or other school employees' cakes. Then ask the adults to see if the children's estimates were accurate.

Use the activity page to make math fact or number recognition task cards. Make several copies of the page and write a math fact or numeral on the cake. Have the children arrange the corresponding number of candles on each cake to complete the task.

Make Your Own Birthday Candle

Melt paraffin wax over a double boiler (paraffin can ignite if it gets too hot), or melt wax granules that can be found in craft stores as directed on the package. At this time, you can also add color and scents, as desired, using tints or oils, also available at craft supply stores. Fill a large pan with wet sand. Have each child hollow out a shape in the sand. Tie a wick onto a stick labeled with the child's name and place it over the impression in the sand so that the wick is centered over the mold and extends down into it. Pour the hot wax (adults only) into each mold, then let the candles sit until the wax has cooled and set.

Un-Birthday Wishes

Make a copy of page 12 for each child. Let the children color the page and draw pictures of the wishes they would make if it were their real birthdays. If appropriate, record their ideas on the papers and read them back to the children when you have finished.

10

Counting Candles

There are ___ candles on the cake.

Un-Birthday Wishes

Pancake Day

Whether you prefer flapjacks, hot cakes, pancakes, or a short stack,
Pancake Day is a holiday you can really flip over!

Pancake Pileup

Make a large number of small pancakes 2"–3" (51–76 mm) in diameter. Let the children count as they stack the pancakes on top of one another. How high can you build it before it tumbles?

Variation: Measure an average sized pancake. Use this measurement to create several pancake patterns out of tagboard. Use the paper shape to measure distances such as, "It is _____ pancakes from the classroom door to the drinking fountain."

Face Flapjacks

Make a large batch of pancake batter using a complete mix or your favorite recipe. Thin with milk until the batter can be easily poured from a spoon or measuring cup. Reserve one third of the batter in another bowl

and tint it with food coloring. Make face pancakes by pouring two small circles of the colored batter in the middle of a hot frying pan, and another thin line below to create a "smiley" face. Cook until bubbles begin to form on top of the eyes and mouth. Pour a circle of plain batter around the outside of these features, then fill in the circle with more batter. When the batter begins to form bubbles that pop, flip the pancake to reveal a face! When finished cooking, serve the flapjacks with syrup for a delicious treat.

Pancake Pounce

Cut large circles (approximately 8"–10" or 20–25 cm in diameter) of plain heavy paper. Write numbers, alphabet letters, color words, blends, words to rhyme or draw shapes on the circle, one word/picture on each. Tape the circles randomly on the floor. Let the children take turns jumping from one "pancake" to another as you call out the words, numbers, or math equations (e.g., All the children should jump to a "pancake" with the number "6" when you call out: "Jump to 1 + 5").

Syrup Art

Fill three bowls with clear corn syrup. Color one bowl of syrup blue, one bowl red, and the third one yellow using a generous amount of food coloring. Let each child create designs by drizzling syrup from a spoon onto a white piece of paper or paper plate. Be sure to cover the table with newspaper and the child with a smock before beginning this activity.

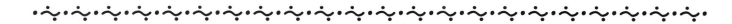

Pancake Prance

Divide the class into teams. Give each team a spatula and a cardboard "pancake." The object of the game is for each member to run or walk to one end of the room and back to the starting point without loosing the "pancake" off the spatula. (If you drop your pancake mid-race, you must return to the beginning and start over.) The first team to complete the race is declared the "Ultimate Pancake Porters." Mix the teams and play again as time and interest allows.

Variation: Make the race more challenging by having the children hop on one foot, walk backwards, or follow the voice of a teammate through a short obstacle course while blindfolded.

Flapjack Jake Face Flip

Color the activity page of Flapjack Jake and laminate for durability. Hang a tarp or large sheet of paper on an outside wall. Tape "Flapjack Jake" to the tarp. Prepare a batch of small "pancakes" 2"–3" (51–76 mm) in diameter by cutting the shapes from tagboard. Provide at least one cutout for each child. Mark a line about 3'–4' (92–120 cm) in front of "Flapjack Jake," or place a hula hoop on the ground as a "launching area." Using a flexible spatula, let each child take turns flipping a shaving cream-covered "pancake" at Flapjack Jake's face to see who can hit him squarely on the nose.

Pancake Shape Match

Discuss with the children what shape pancakes are. Send the children on a scavenger hunt around the classroom to bring back items or pictures of objects that match the shape of a pancake. Count and compare the collected items. If several identical objects are found, arrange the items on a large floor graphing mat to show which object is the most popular choice.

Story Time

Share the story *Pancakes, Pancakes!* by Eric Carle (Picture Studio, 1989) with the children. To extend the story into your lesson, make pancakes as you read along in the book. After reading the story, have the children return to their seats and see how many steps of the pancake-making process they can remember from the story.

Variation: Have the children write their own pancake recipes including ingredients and instructions for making the pancakes from start to finish. Be sure the children illustrate themselves enjoying their recipe creations.

IF01366 Holidays for Dull Days

Friendship Week

Big, small, short, tall; friends come in all shapes and sizes.
Celebrate Friendship Week with them all.

Guess Which Friend?

During playtime, move about the room capturing the children's voices on audio tape. Be sure to get a clear recording of each child. At group time, play the recordings and have the children identify which friend is talking on the tape.

Musical Friends

Play musical friends by turning on marching or dancing music. Instruct the children to move about the room to the music, but when the music stops each child must find a friend and do as the teacher says. For instance: give a gentle hug, handshakes, bear hugs, "high fives," wink at your friend, etc. Be sure to encourage each child to find a new friend each time the music stops.

Variations: Give each child an index card with a math equation or the solution to the equation (rhyming words, beginning sounds, etc., can also be used). For example, one child is given a card with "2 + 9 =" written on it, and another child is given the card showing "11." When the music stops, the child must find the friend that holds the corresponding card.

When the music stops, call out a number such as "5." The children must assemble themselves into groups of five in a hug. Repeat until the children are ready to end the game.

Friends . . .

Get a large sheet of butcher paper and write "Friends . . ." at the top. Ask the children to describe a friend and list their responses on the paper. If appropriate, write the words for them.

Extension: Write each child's name on a slip of paper. Invite each child to draw one of the slips and make a special picture for this classroom friend (give child a copy of page 20). When finished, encourage the child to complete the sentence "I like you because . . ." Share these special thoughts about the children at group time.

Is This Person Being a Good Friend?

Use the picture cards on pages 17-19 (or search magazines or newspapers for pictures) depicting children in activities that display actions that demonstrate being good friends or not being good friends. Talk about what being a good friend means, and include concrete ideas of how to make new friends and resolve differences.

Variation: Have the children form small groups, then give each group a different scenario that depicts someone not acting in a friendly way. Have the children role-play the situation and any ideas for conflict resolution for the whole class.

Friendship Collage

Send home with each child a copy of the Friendship Collage note on page 21 a few days before doing this activity. Make a copy of the Friendship Collage activity page for each child. Have the children share their items with each other and then glue the items on their papers.

I Am a Good Friend when . . .

Make a copy of the activity sheet on page 22 for each child. Have the children draw pictures of things they can do to be a good friend to others. If appropriate, record their responses and read them back to the children.

Friendship Chain

Copy page 23 so that there is one figure for each child. Have the children color, add hair, and write their names on the figures. Using the figures, make a friendship chain on the wall or bulletin board by taping the figures with overlapping hands.

Is This Person Being a Good Friend?

Copy and color as desired, then cut apart the cards.

Is This Person Being a Good Friend?

Copy and color as desired, then cut apart the cards.

Is This Person Being a Good Friend?

Copy and color as desired, then cut apart the cards.

Friendship Collage Note

Dear Parents/Guardians,

On _____ we will be creating friendship collages as a class. Please help your child choose some small items such as paper clips, pennies, noodles, cereal, leaves, etc., to share with each child in the class. There are _____ children in our class.

Sincerely,

I like you because

Friendship Collage

IF01366 Holidays for Dull Days

I am a good friend when . . .

Pig Day

There will be nothing but fun with these Pig Day activities.

Piggy Snouts

Cut cardboard tubes into 2" (51 mm) lengths. Cover each tube with pink construction paper and secure with glue. Cut out a circle slightly larger than the diameter of the cardboard tube from pink construction paper. Draw two small dark circles on the pink circle. Squeeze a line of glue around the edge of the cardboard tube and glue the tube to the back of the pink circle. Punch a hole on each side of the cardboard tube. Tie a 12" (305 mm) string to each hole, then try on your snout.

Mud Hide and Seek

Fill a large, flat container with chocolate pudding (mud may also be used if desired). Place several small plastic toys into the pudding/mud and stir to hide the objects. Wearing protective smocks, have the children sink their hands into the "mud" to try to find the hidden toys. Be sure to cover your work area with newspaper or plastic, and provide a bucket of soapy water and towels for a quick cleanup to contain the mud mess to a minimum.

Variation: Prepare index cards with words that describe the hidden objects such as blue, soft, animal, etc. Have the child choose two or three cards and then find an object in the mud that matches each characteristic. For example, if the child pulls a yellow bus out of the mud and the card states "blue," the child must return the bus and continue searching for a match.

Put the Snout on the Piggy

Prepare a "snout" for each child by cutting a circle (approximately 1½" or 38 mm in diameter) of pink paper. Copy the Put the Snout on the Piggy pattern page and color the pig as desired and laminate for durability. Blindfold each child in turn and let him/her try to tape the "snout" on Piggy.

Variation: Have each child write a word that rhymes with "pig" on the snout before playing the game. After everyone has had a turn, tally the answers that are similar to see which rhyming word was used the most times. Repeat with other "pig" words such as hog, slop, pink.

Oink Opposites

Choose one child to be the "Big Pig." (If interested, have the child wear the Big Pig Mask, pattern provided on page 27.) Select an action that the children can perform, such as standing up. When Big Pig says "oink" once, the children should stand up. When Big Pig says "oink, oink," the children should sit down. The child who follows Big Pig's directions the best gets to be the next Big Pig and choose another activity for the children to follow.

Variation: Prepare word cards for working on the concept of "opposites." Write one of an "opposite" pair on each card, such as hot/cold, day/night, big/little, thick/thin, up/down, above/below, summer/winter, etc. Have Big Pig say the word on one of the cards. The other children must say a word that has an opposite meaning to earn a game point.

Eat Like a Pig

Place a muffin on a napkin in front of each seated child. Remind the children that this is the one time that eating like a pig is appropriate. Have the children sit with their hands behind their backs or in their laps while they "eat like a pig."

Pink Pig Tail Painting

Place pink paint in a pan. Cut a 10" (25 cm) length of rope and attach a clothespin to one end. Let the children paint with their "pig tails" by holding the clothespins and dipping the "pig tails" in the pink paint and then stroking their papers with the tails.

Pig Tag

Cut a 12" (30 cm) length of rope for each child. (It works well to make the tails in two different colors.) Have the children form two teams and then spread out to be at least an arm's length away from another player in a large open area. Tuck the end of the rope into the back pocket of each child's pants or secure it to the back of the child's clothing with a clothespin so that each child has a "piggy tail." At your command, the children then race to see how many pig tails they can confiscate from the other team's players. Use the pig tails to measure distances. For example, Team 1 collected 12 piggy tails which can reach 12' (3.6 m). The first team to gather enough piggy tails to reach across a predetermined distance is the winner. This may take more than one game to complete so combine totals to reach the grand total.

Variation: Create a math sentence by subtracting the number of pig tails collected by one team from the total number of players to get the number collected by the second team. (When the students check their answer, the numbers must add up to the total number of players.)

Animals on the Farm

How many pigs are in the barnyard? How many animals can you see? To create fun file folder activities, copy the patterns on pages 28–29, one or more copies per file folder. Decide how many animals will be pictured in each scene. For example, to show a set of four pigs, glue the barnyard in place on the file folder, then glue four pigs in random order. Complete the scene by including other animals for the children to count and the box for recording the number of pigs/animals shown in the scene. Color the pictures and then laminate the file folder for durability. Let the child use a watercolor marker to write how many animals/pigs are shown in the barnyard. When finished, wipe off the numeral with a damp cloth.

Variation: If appropriate, have the children write math sentences about the scenes.

Story Time

Share the story *Pigs* by Robert Munsch (Annick Press, 1989). Have the children tell which parts of the story they enjoyed the most.

Extension: Have each child write a short story imagining that the pigs in the story are now running through the classroom, house, school bus, or another location.

Animals on the Farm

Color and cut out the animals. Glue them to the picture of the barnyard.

National Noodle Month

Whether it is spaghetti, macaroni and cheese, or chicken noodle soup,
many people enjoy noodles every day.
Celebrate National Noodle Month and learn to appreciate the noodle in a different way!

Noodle Necklaces

Gather noodles with wide openings for this activity. Add several drops of food coloring to a small amount of rubbing alcohol. Place several handfuls of noodles and the colored mixture in a tightly sealed container. Shake. Repeat for a deeper color if desired. Place the colored noodles on a sheet of waxed paper to air-dry, turning them occasionally.

Cut a 24" (61 cm) length of yarn or string for each child. Tie a noodle to one end, then tape the other loose end to make a needle for stringing the noodles. Encourage the children to create colorful necklaces that can be worn.

Variation: Use the different colored noodles to create patterns when forming the necklaces. If appropriate, start the pattern on the string for the child to complete.

Use Your Noodle

How many noodles to the bathroom? How many noodles tall are you? Fill in the noodle measuring chart (make a copy of page 33 for each child) by measuring the length or distance using a spaghetti noodle. This activity is great for cooperating with a friend in your measuring excursion!

Kaboodles of Noodles

Place a large assortment of noodles in a bowl in the middle of the table. Give each child the Kaboodles of Noodles graphing sheet copied on heavy cardstock. Have the children begin the project by gluing one of each variety of noodles in a left-hand space on the grid. Now take a small handful of noodles from the bowl, sort the noodles, and glue them in the appropriate squares. If the row of squares is filled, return the unused noodles to the container and then count the noodles shown on the chart.

Variation: Color the noodles (as suggested in the noodle necklace activity), then let the children sort the noodles by size, color, or type of pasta.

Noodle Doodles

Place a large assortment of noodles in a bowl in the middle of the table. Give each child a piece of colored construction paper and glue. Encourage the children to use their imaginations to create pictures by arranging the noodles on their papers. Be sure to allow enough time for the work to dry before moving the masterpieces. If appropriate, have the students write short stories about their pictures. Display the stories with the pictures.

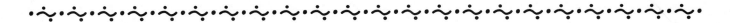

Variation: Create a small wall hanging with noodles for a special gift. To prepare the material, dip a square piece of burlap in liquid starch. Cut a length of string and tie it in a loop. Place the string across the top of the burlap and then fold the edge over the string to hold it in place. (The string will be used to hang the picture when it is completed.) Allow the burlap to dry overnight. To finish the wall hanging, glue various colored and plain noodles on the burlap canvas to create a work of art ready to be hung in any gallery.

Noodle Numbering

Fill a clear jar or container with an assortment of noodles. Have the children guess how many different kinds of noodles are found in the jar, and then estimate the number of each variety.

Once all the children have had an opportunity to guess or estimate, pour the noodles out and count to see if anyone was right on the noodle!

Variation: Use several different sizes of containers filled with the same type of noodles. Have the children estimate the number of noodles in each jar. When finished, give each group a small cup of 10 noodles. Use this amount as a strategy to help the children arrive at a close estimate for the actual number of noodles in each jar. Using noodles from the jar, have the children fill additional small cups to match the sample cup. When the jar is empty, have the children count how many cups have been filled and count by 10s to arrive at a reasonable estimate.

Noodle Tracks

Cook a package of spaghetti noodles so that they are soft and flexible, yet still firm enough to handle. (You may also color the noodles by adding several drops of food coloring to the boiling water with the raw noodles.) Drain and cool. Tape a large sheet of butcher paper to a table, then draw several simple line drawings with a marker on the paper. Have the children try to trace the noodle tracks by placing the noodles along the lines.

Variation: Instead of shapes, write words, letters, or numbers for the children to trace with noodles. If interested, the children can form their names with noodles. Once the noodles have air-dried, they will hold their forms and can be glued onto another sheet of paper.

Egg Noodles

2 c. (474 ml) flour
3 egg yolks
1 egg
1½ tsp. (7.5 ml) salt
water

Mix together the flour, salt, egg yolks, and egg. Mix in water 1 tbsp. (15 ml) at a time until the dough is stiff but rolls easily.

Roll dough paper thin on a cloth-covered board (flour generously). Cut into strips ¼" (6 mm) thick and place on a towel until dry (about 2 hours). To cook: Break into smaller pieces, cook in boiling water 12–15 minutes.

If interested, use a noodle maker to cut and shape your noodles. Serve the homemade noodles with pasta sauce.

Noodle Matching Game

Make four copies of the Noodle Matching Game cards on colored cardstock or copy on white cardstock and color each noodle card separately. Cut out the cards and laminate them for durability. To play the matching game, place all cards face down and take turns turning over two cards at a time. If a match is made, the child collects the pair and gets another turn. If no match is made, play resumes with the next child.

Use Your Noodle

Use your spaghetti to measure lengths and distances.

 1. My finger is _____ noodles long.

 2. My shoes are _____ noodles long.

 3. I am _____ noodles tall.

 4. The table is _____ noodles wide.

 5. My arm is _____ noodles long.

6. It is _____ noodles to the window.

7. A crayon is _____ noodles long.

 8. My favorite toy is _____ noodles long.

 9. It is _____ noodles to the bathroom.

 10. My teacher is _____ noodles tall.

Kaboodles of Noodles

Garden Month

Even if you do not grow vegetables, flowers, herbs, or fruits in beds, windowsills, pots, or plots, these easy-to-do Garden Month activities will surely give you a green thumb.

Plant Walk

Take your children on a nature walk to explore all the different plants found in their neighborhood. If possible, gather a few samples to take back to the classroom for comparing and contrasting experiences. Be sure to explore plants with different colors, textures, and sizes. Using magnifying glasses, the children can make great observations.

Variation: Make a small booklet of blank pages for each child to use on the nature walk. The children can then make rubbings of leaves, trace leaves or blossoms, and take notes about the plants they find by writing descriptive words or recording other observations in their nature books.

Paint and Pot a Plant

Use tempera or acrylic paints to decorate a ceramic pot. Seal the inside and outside of the pot with acrylic finish. Fill the pot with potting soil and plant seeds (marigolds show results quickly) or seedlings in the dirt. Place the pot in a window and watch your garden grow.

Extension: Have the children keep journals about their potted plants by charting the growth (stems can be measured every few days, the number of leaves counted and graphed, new buds noted), or other changes they observe during their green thumb ventures.

Growing Veggies

You can grow plants from several different vegetables with little more than water and sunlight. Grow your own garden right in the classroom by poking toothpicks into a sweet potato near the top of the vegetable. Fill a jar with water and rest the toothpicks on the rim of the jar so that the bottom half of the potato is immersed in water. Place the jar in a sunny spot; watch for a new leafy vine to sprout in a few days.

Variation: Try this activity with other vegetables, such as carrots, potatoes, turnips, etc. Compare and contrast the results (or lack thereof) of your indoor garden. "Which plant grew most or least?" "How are the leaves different?" "Which needed the most water for growth?"

Making Seed Patterns

Colorful, shapely patterns can be made with seeds—several different kinds of beans, sunflower seeds, large flower seeds, and so on. Just locate interesting seeds and make a copy of the activity sheet on page 38. Color the grid sheet as desired and mount it on a file folder or construction paper. Laminate the sheet for durability. You may wish to prepare several activity sheets for the children to use. To help the children get started, tape a few seeds in place to begin patterns for the children to finish, such as ABBA, ABAB, and ABCABC patterns.

35

Web of Worms

Cut several strands of yarn in a variety of lengths 2"–12" (51–305 mm). Have the child dip the yarn strands into liquid starch until saturated, then arrange the yarn "worms" on a piece of paper and allow them to air-dry.

Variation: Place the yarn "worms" on waxed paper in order from shortest to longest length, then set aside to dry.

Wiggly Worms

Draw a small face on each child's index finger with a nontoxic washable marker. Have the children wiggle their "worms" high, low, behind their backs, on top of their heads, and other different ways.

Variation: Encourage the children to act out the life cycle of a seed. Choose some of the children to be seeds, another group to be the sun, more to be rain, and so on. As the children "grow," have them move from crouching to standing with arms outstretched, as the leaves bud out and grow.

Growing Seeds

Discuss with the class the steps needed to grow a garden (e.g., The weather must be warm; seeds need soil, water, and sun). Soak lima beans overnight in water so the seed coats are soft and slide off easily. Working in pairs, have the children plant several lima beans in clear plastic glasses, partially filled with potting soil. Place the beans next to the glass. Observe the plant growth, noting that regardless of the orientation of the seed, the roots always grow down and the plant always grows up.

Variation: Plant other quickly germinating seeds such as radish or rye grass. Compare and contrast the plants and their leaves.

Bean Experiments

Lima beans (or bush beans) are simple to grow and produce results quickly. Fill five cups with potting dirt, then plant two or three beans in each one. Talk about how plants need water, sunlight, and warm soil to grow. To demonstrate this concept, perform the following experiments and mark the progress of your "gardens" over the next week.

1. Place one cup in a sunny window and a second cup inside a box or a dark cabinet. Water as needed.
2. Place a third cup in the freezer.
3. Label a fourth cup "no water" and place it with the other cup in the window. Do not water this cup.
4. Empty the dirt from a fifth cup and place the beans in the cup without dirt. Place the cup on the windowsill with the other cups and water daily.

Gardener's Headband

Make one copy of page 37 for each child. Prepare a headband by cutting a piece of construction paper in thirds lengthwise. Staple two strips of paper together to make one long headband strip. Have the child color and cut out the garden objects  and glue them to the headband. The children may enjoy wearing their headbands during the Paint and Pot a Plant activity.

Gardener's Headband

Make one copy of this page for each child. Prepare a headband by cutting a piece of construction paper in thirds lengthwise. Staple two strips of paper together to make one long strip. Have the child color and cut out the objects and glue them to the headband.

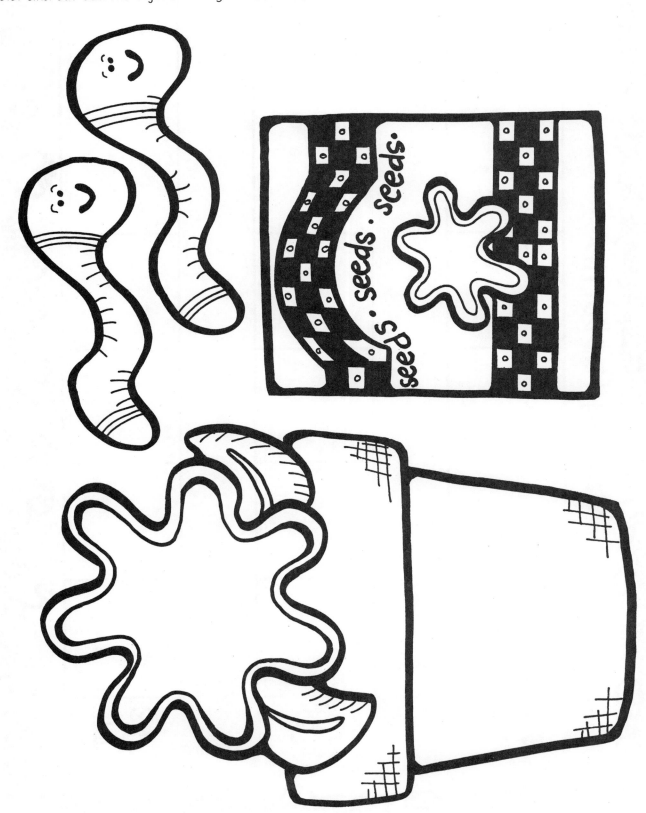

37

Making Patterns

IF01366 Holidays for Dull Days

Astronomy Day

Astronomy is the study of stars and planets.
As an astronomer, you can discover your own comet, explore a black hole, or map out the next galaxy.
Whatever you choose, celebrating Astronomy Day is sure to be out of this world!

Space Helmets

Cut the top off a large paper bag so that it fits over a child's head and rests on his/her shoulders. Cut a hole in the front side of the bag as shown. Cut a similar hole through a paper plate. Color the bag and plate as desired. Glue the plate to the bag matching the holes.

Star Dancing

Cut a star from construction paper for each child, then punch a hole in the top of each star shape. Tie a 24" (61 cm) length of string to the star through the hole. Play a music tape (you may use theme music such as "Star Wars" or any lively movement music) and let the children dance and move pulling the star on a string behind them.

Rocket to the Moon

Secure a string to the ceiling or another high point in the room. Make a copy of the Rocket to the Moon pattern page and cut out the pictures. Tape the moon at the end of the string. Tape a drinking straw securely to the back of the rocket. Thread the string through the drinking straw and tack the bottom of the string to the floor with masking tape (make sure the string is tight). Inflate a 9" (23 cm) balloon, then pinch the neck of the balloon with a clothespin to keep the air from escaping. Tape the straw to the balloon. Have the

children place their space helmets on their heads and count backwards from 10. Release the clothespin to send the rocket to the moon.

Variation: Have the children predict what the results would be if the rocket activity was altered by using different sizes of balloons to propel the rocket or by changing the angle or length of the string. Remind the children to write down their hypotheses, conduct their trials, and observe and record the results.

Space Walk

Once you have reached the moon, carefully climb out of the spacecraft and pretend to walk on the moon. Point out interesting moon rocks and other formations. Remember there is no gravity on the moon so that walking requires heavy shoes, and great effort. This is a great time to wear your space helmet!

Extension: Read *Mooncake* by Frank Asche (Prentice-Hall, 1983). Expand on the ideas in the book by making your own shaved ice treats by crushing ice and water in a blender until the mixture is slushy. Add presweetened drink mix powder to taste for flavoring. Practice counting backwards and "blasting off" by allowing the children to jump up from a crouched position each time you reach "0." If appropriate, count backwards from 100 by 10s, 50 by 5s, etc.

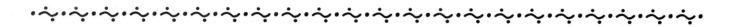

Space Drink

6 oz. (180 ml) frozen juice concentrate
(any flavor)
1 c. (240 ml) milk
1 c. (240 ml) water
15 ice cubes
½ c. (118 ml) ice cream

Crush the ice cubes in a blender. Mix the remaining ingredients until smooth. (Add more milk if a thinner consistency is desired.) Pour the mixture into small resealable sandwich bags. Poke a straw through the side of each bag near the top and enjoy drinking your juice from a bag like the astronauts!

Twinkle, Twinkle

Sing "Twinkle, Twinkle, Little Star" as a class. Then sing it again, experimenting with the tempo of the song by singing it as fast and then as slowly as you can. Next, try altering the pitch by singing high and then low. Sing one more time softly and then loudly. Can you think of other ways this song can be sung?

Stuffed Stars

Cut large star shapes out of butcher or craft paper, two for each child. Staple the edges, or punch holes around the edges and lace them together by weaving a length of yarn through the holes. Leave one side of the star open. Color or paint the star as desired. Stuff the inside with crumpled newspaper scraps. Finish lacing or stapling the star's edges. Hang the children's creations from the ceiling to create your own classroom Milky Way.

Variation: Show the children pictures of the Milky Way and introduce the concept of galaxy.

Constellations

Tape a large sheet of butcher paper to a table. Draw many stars randomly on the paper. Let the children practice their eye-hand coordination by connecting the stars and creating their own constellations.

Variation: Use the constellation cards (see page 43) to draw constellations on the sheet of butcher paper. Let the children use the cards to identify each constellation drawn. Encourage the children to take home a set of the cards to see if they can find one or more of the constellations in the night sky.

Astronomy Mobile

Collect clothes hangers, one for each child. Make a copy of the Astronomy Mobile pattern page for each child. Have the child color and cut out the space shapes, and punch a hole in the top of each where indicated by a small circle. Cut four lengths of string for each child. Tie the shapes to the hanger with string to create a celestial mobile!

Our Sun, A Special Star

There is one star in the sky that gives us bright light—our sun which is the closest star to Earth. To show how this happens, remove the shade from a small lamp and place the lamp on the floor where the children can see it. Select a small ball to represent Earth. (You may want to explain that the sun is actually much larger than Earth, but you are using these props for today's discussion.) Turn the lamp on and show the children how the sun (or light) brightens one side of the ball (or Earth) at a time. This is called "day." The side that is away from the sun is dark. This is called "night." Draw a small "x" on the ball. Explain that this is where we live on Earth. Rotate the ball showing how the "x" faces the light sometimes and faces away from the light at other times, just like we have day and night, respectively. Ask your children to predict what people who live on the opposite side of Earth are doing when the children are sleeping.

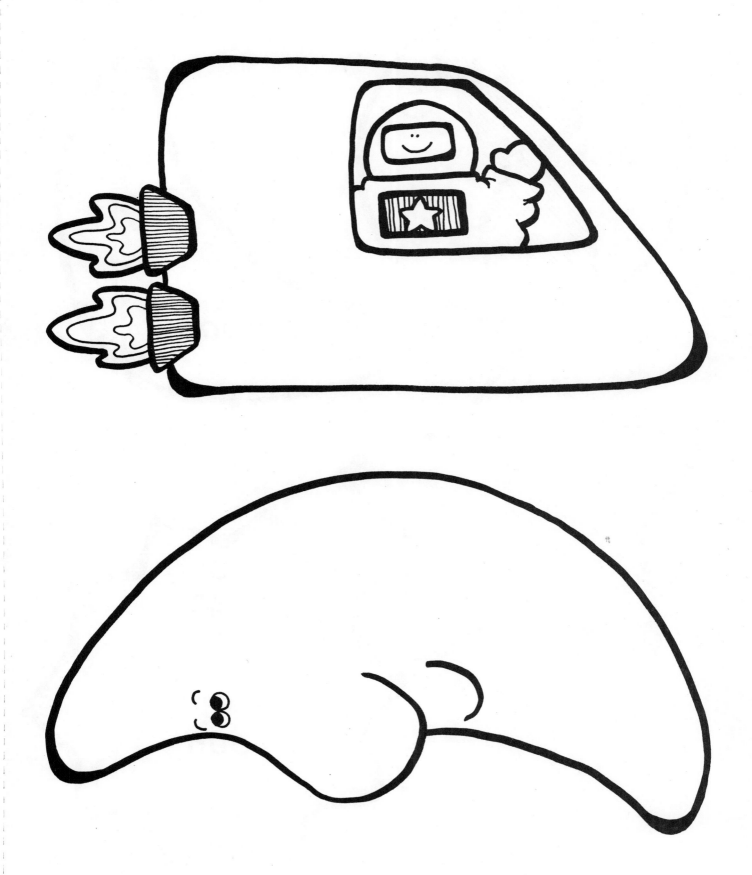

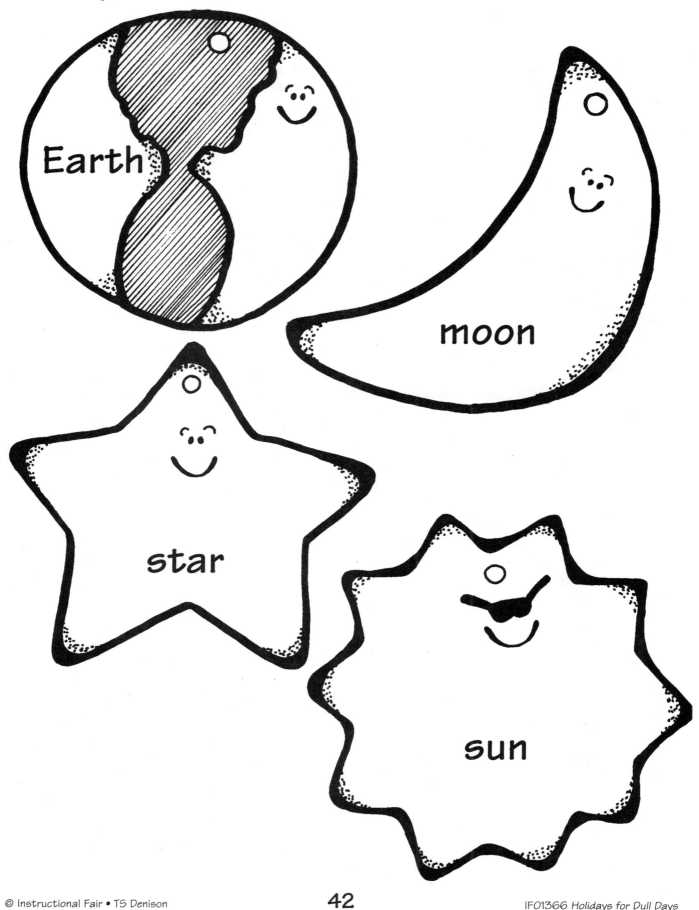

Constellations

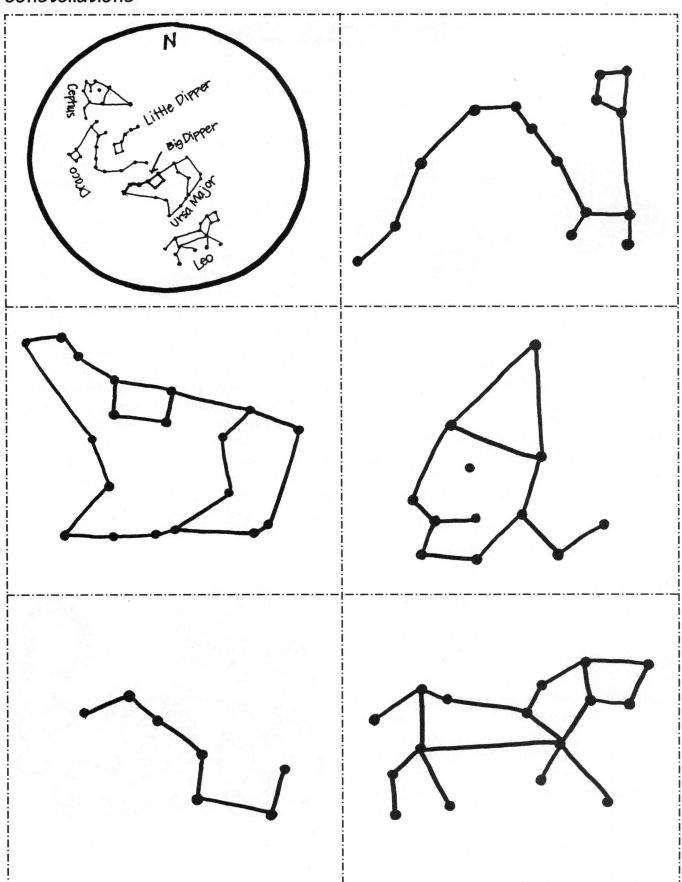

No Socks Day

*People wear socks for comfort, fashion, and protection.
Here is a day of celebration to knock your socks off!*

Crazy Socks Contest

A few days before celebrating this holiday, send home a note asking parents to help their children prepare for a "Crazy Socks Contest." Children should search their homes for unusual socks to wear, or encourage the children to create their own crazy socks by decorating them. Host a crazy sock parade to show off the unique socks the children are wearing. Give an award for the craziest pair, most unique, and so on.

Sock Toss

Make simple bean bags by filling socks with dried beans or rice and tying knots at the top of the socks to keep the contents inside. Draw a target on a piece of paper or chalkboard, and take your aim.

Variation: Have the children fill their own socks using measuring, weighing, and balancing skills. "Can you fill two socks with identical weights?" Try using different ingredients. "Does it take the same amount of rice as it does beans to make the bean bags equal in weight?" Next chart whether socks filled with fewer beans can be thrown farther than socks with a greater amount of beans. Measure the distance the children can toss the socks. Award first, second, and third place to the socks that travel the farthest distances respectively.

Sock-It-to-Me

Gather six different colored socks. Color a sock on the Sock-It-to-Me wheel (see page 46) to correspond with each color of sock you have gathered. Laminate the game board for durability if desired. On small slips of paper, write down activities ("Jump up and down 10 times," "Sing your favorite song"), word associations (cat:kitten, dog:?), math problems, or review questions about units you are currently covering in class. Insert several different slips into each sock.

Have the children take turns spinning the wheel. To make the spinner, place a pencil point through a large paper clip, then press the tip of the pencil into the dot in the center of the wheel. Flick the paper clip with your finger to make it spin around the wheel. When the paper clip points to a sock, select the matching colored sock and pull out one slip of paper. Have all children perform the task written on the piece of paper. Continue playing the game until each child has had a turn.

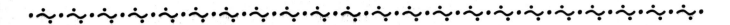

No Socks Painting

Prepare the painting surface by laying newspaper or a large tarp on the floor. Fill a large, flat pan with tempera paint. Have a bucket of soapy water and towels ready for cleanup. Let each child paint using his/her bare feet on a large sheet of butcher paper. *Caution:* Paint can be very slippery, use a chair or a helper to keep painters from painting their backsides, too!

Sock On/Sock Off

Explore your environment by taking a walk indoors and outdoors (weather permitting) with one sock on your foot and the other sock off. Talk about the differences in texture and temperature that your feet feel.

All Kinds of Socks

Gather an assortment of different kinds of socks. You should include a wide variety such as warm woolen socks, nylon stockings, athletic socks, trouser socks, and anklets. Place the socks into a brown paper bag and have the children take turns selecting socks from the bag. Talk about texture, size, color, and when or where the sock should be appropriately worn.

Variation: Send a note to parents encouraging the children to bring in a few socks from home (label by pinning the child's name on a slip of paper inside the sock with a safety pin). Encourage the children to not only bring in a variety of colors but also patterns, prints, sizes, and styles. Let the children sort by colors, patterns, sizes, textures, or other characteristics. You may wish to graph the results by arranging the socks on a large floor graphing mat.

Sock Puppets

Ask parents to donate stray or mismatched socks for making sock puppets. Use wiggly craft eyes, felt, yarn, or the features included on the Sock Puppet Features  page to create your own sock masterpieces.

When your sock puppets are ready for use, choose a simple story (or create one) to put on your own puppet show. You can make a simple theater by turning a table on its side or by placing a long tablecloth or sheet between two chairs. After practicing, take your puppet show on tour and travel to entertain other classrooms.

Sock Blast

Take a large number of socks and roll them into balls. To divide the playing area in half, place a line of masking tape or arrange some other marker across the middle of the room. Separate the class into two teams. The object of this game is to see which team can get the most socks on the opposing team's side by tossing the socks over the line. Set a timer for 3–5 minutes and begin the game. Have the children count the socks when time is up to determine the winning team.

Variation: Before beginning the game, count the total number of socks to be used. After the time has signaled the end of the game, count the number of socks on each side of the room. Write the results as a math sentence on a large sheet of paper. For example, if the game started with 25 socks and one team collected 12 socks, the math sentence is written as "25 − 12 = 13." The children on the other team should check to be sure they have 13 socks. If they do not have that total, they may have to search for a lost sock or recount the socks. Each time the children play a round, there will be a different math sentence to record.

Sock-It-to-Me

IF01366 Holidays for Dull Days

Sock Puppet Features

Family Day

Grandparents, siblings, and parents, too, this day of family fun would not be possible without you!

Family Show and Tell

Send home the parent note included at the end of this lesson with each child, encouraging him/her to bring a current family photograph for a family "Show and Tell." Let the children show pictures of their families, identify the people in the pictures, and relate their favorite things to do with people who are meaningful to them.

Family Faces Graph

Make enough copies of the Family Faces Graph pattern page so that you have enough parents/guardians and siblings to represent the families of the children in your class. Separate the faces so that all of the males are in one envelope, all the females in another, and so on. On a large sheet of paper or poster board, glue one of each family face along the short side of the paper as shown. Let each child choose the family faces that represent his/her family from the envelopes, and tape the pictures to the board in the appropriate rows. Once all the children have had the opportunity to add their family faces, count the total number of fathers, mothers, brothers, sisters, and other special family members.

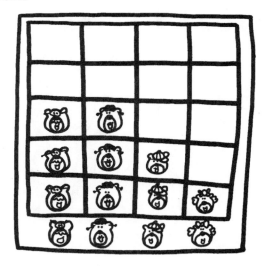

Dress Up

Provide an assortment of adult-sized dress-up clothes as well as a full-length mirror for the children to play dress up. Be sure to include hats, shoes, and other accessories in addition to the clothing. You may also want to offer the opportunity to "shave" with shaving cream and a Popsicle or craft stick for a razor, or to put on make-up with face paints.

Family Portrait

Have each child draw a portrait of his/her family members. You may want to offer several different media such as crayons, pastels, markers, colored pencils, chalk, and an assortment of collage materials for the children to use in creating their pictures. Help the child label the people in his/her picture. Mount the picture on colored construction paper.

Mom and Dad Show and Tell

Invite at least one mom and dad volunteer to come and "show and tell" what they do all day. Encourage parents to bring props that they use in their work for the children to view or experience.

Variation: Make a copy of page 52 for each child. Ask each child what his/her parents do during the day while they are away. Have the children finish the activity page. Parents will find it particularly enlightening to find out what their children really think they do all day.

Mom and Dad Favorites

Let the children color or draw pictures of their favorite things to do with their parents on the Mom and Dad Favorites activity page provided at the end of this lesson. Have the child dictate his/her thoughts to you as you write them on the paper. Be sure to read the words back to the child.

Story Time

Read *What Is a Family?* and *What Kind of Family Do You Have?* by Gretchen Super (Twenty-first Century Publishers, 1991). Explain that a family is people who love one another, who take care of one another, and who do things together. Use the ideas presented in the books to discuss different kinds of families (including blended, adoptive, foster, extended, and nuclear families), how we are all different, and how each family's differences make it unique and interesting.

Extension: Locate several books about families living in different cultures. Talk about how families' customs and traditions are different around the world.

Circle of Love

Cut many hearts from construction paper (any color—about 3" [76 mm] in diameter) and punch a small hole in the top of each heart. Let the children write or  dictate the names of their family members and write them on the paper hearts. (This can include as many as the children would like to mention on the hearts, such as parents/guardians, pets, cousins, caregivers, grandparents, and others.) Provide a length of string, the hearts, cut pieces of straws, noodles, or other small objects that can be strung into a necklace of love.

Family Tag

Select a large open area for this game. Choose two or three persons to be "Family Starters." At your signal the "Family Starters" who are "It" begin running and attempt to tag other class members to become a part of their "families." Once the person has been tagged, he/she must then join hands with the other "family members" and the chain continues to collect family members by tagging them. (Only the "Family Starter" can tag the next member to join the chain, the others must follow the "Family Starter.") Continue playing until all the children have been tagged. If desired, compare to find out which family is the largest and which one is the smallest. Repeat the game as interest and time allow.

Family Vacations

Send home a note requesting that each child bring a photo, postcard, or other representation of a recent family vacation (this could include a trip to the park or a trip across the globe). Make sure to have the parents label the photo, and remind them that you will be borrowing the photos for a class display for a couple of weeks. Have the parents write a short description of the place they visited so that you can pinpoint the location on a map. Have a large map of the world posted on a bulletin board. As the children bring in their pictures, have them share (or write short stories) about their family vacations including details such as what their favorite activities were, who they sat next to when they traveled, whether they traveled by airplane, train, bus, car, or other form of transportation, and interesting things they observed. Place a small star or sticker over the location where each child's family vacationed. Attach the photo to the bulletin board and secure a piece of yarn from the photo to the location on the map. At the end of the week examine all the different places (near and far) that the children have traveled with their families.

Dear Parents/Guardians,

On _____ we will be having a special "Family Show and Tell." Each child will have an opportunity to show a picture of his/her family and share a little about family members. Please send a picture of your family with your child on this day.

Sincerely,

Dear Parents/Guardians,

To celebrate Family Day, we will be talking about family vacations. We need your help! Will you please provide a photograph of a recent vacation? Please include a short description about the place you visited. Your vacation spot can be a trip to a park or to a different part of our country.

I will need the item by _____. I will be displaying the photograph for a few days and then will take great care in returning it to you. Thanks for your help.

Sincerely,

51

My dad _____

all day.

He works

My mom _____

all day.

She works

My favorite thing to do with Dad is . . .

My favorite thing to do with Mom is . . .

Dairy Month

It's the dairy's job to create cheese, yogurt, butter, and ice cream from milk.
It's your job to enjoy these Dairy Month activities.

Milk the Cow

Draw a simple cow on the side of a cardboard box, or make a copy of the pattern on page 57 and glue it to the side of a box. Cut a small hole ½" (13 mm) in diameter in the bottom of the box. Place the box on and between two tables or chairs and place heavy weights (such as bricks) inside the box. Place a large towel and bucket on the floor underneath the box. Poke small holes in the fingertips of a rubber glove and fill with milk. Tie a knot at the top of the glove and insert it through the hole in the bottom of the box so that the glove fingers are hanging below the box to make a cow's udder. Tape the top of the glove securely inside the bottom of the box with strong packing or duct tape. Let the children take turns "milking" the cow by squeezing and carefully pulling on the fingers to squirt milk into the bucket.

Extension: Talk about, or have the children research the steps for bringing milk from the dairy farm to the grocery store. Use The Story of Milk pattern page to illustrate each step. Make a copy of the picture cards for each child. Let them color, cut out, and assemble the cards in order on sheets of paper.

Milk Shake/Shake Off

A great game for getting the wiggles out! Have all the children stand in a large area where they have room to move their arms and legs without touching another child. When the teacher calls "milk shake," the children should shake every moveable part of their bodies until the teacher calls "shake off." The children should stand absolutely still at this point. Repeat many times.

Butter

You can make your own butter in one large container as a class or individually by using baby food jars. Fill a jar ⅓ full with real whipping cream and seal tightly with a lid. Take turns shaking the container and observing the results as the cream turns from a liquid to a solid mass. As a soft ball of butter begins to form, pour off the excess water, reseal the container and continue shaking until a moderately firm ball forms. Add a pinch of salt and enjoy your homemade butter on a cracker or slice of warm bread.

Cheese Shape Snacks

Cheese is another product made from milk. Using a plastic knife or small cookie cutter, cut out shapes from cheese slices. Be sure to eat your shapes and scraps when you have finished cutting.

Pudding Pops

Mix any 6-oz. (178-ml) flavor pudding with milk as instructed on the package directions. Add 1 cup (237 ml) of whipped topping (or actual cream that has been whipped) and stir. Pour or scoop the mixture into small paper cups and add Popsicle or craft sticks. Place in the freezer until completely frozen. Remove the paper cup and enjoy another delicious treat made possible by milk!

Extension: Try freezing the ingredients separately to see which substance (pudding, whipped topping, or the combination) freezes faster than the others. Use a magnifying glass to observe and compare the ice crystals of each substance. Make predictions about how much time it will take to freeze the pops.

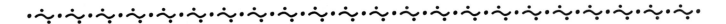

Condensed Milk Paint

Fill each cup of a 6-cup muffin tin with equal amounts of sweetened condensed milk. Add several drops of food coloring to each cup to create six different colors of "milk paint" and stir thoroughly. Place a small paintbrush in each cup. Let the children use the paint to create their own beautiful rainbows on sheets of white paper. Encourage the children to not mix the colors as they paint. Allow the pictures to dry overnight for beautiful results.

Milk Cartons

Gather several sizes of dairy product cartons. Spray paint or cover them with colored paper. Let the children use the cartons as blocks or to create buildings. If appropriate, have the children draw pictures of their buildings to show the front, side, and back views. They can indicate on their pictures how many cartons were used.

Variations: Use the cartons for measuring activities. Provide several identical cartons for measuring distances and lengths of objects. Have the children predict and then measure to find the answers. If children are to compare weights of cartons, fill the selected cartons with water and seal them securely. Provide balances for the children to use when comparing masses (weights). At the water table, young children can fill the cartons with water to explore volume, such as how many pints equal a quart or which container holds more milliliters.

Buttermilk Art

Fill a small bowl with buttermilk. Paint one side of a piece of construction paper with the buttermilk. Use colored chalk to create interesting results in your buttermilk pictures.

Old Bossy

Make a copy of the Old Bossy activity page provided at the end of this lesson for each child. Provide a large assortment of color crayons: be sure to include brown, yellow, green, red, blue, and

pink. Give a copy of "Old Bossy" to each child. Recite the "Old Bossy" poem shown below, pausing before reading the name of the color to see if the children can guess the color by rhyming it with the second line of the stanza. Once the correct color is determined, have each child color "Old Bossy" as indicated and continue the poem.

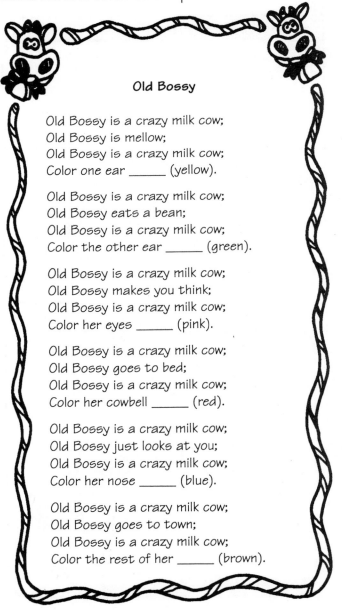

Old Bossy

Old Bossy is a crazy milk cow;
Old Bossy is mellow;
Old Bossy is a crazy milk cow;
Color one ear _____ (yellow).

Old Bossy is a crazy milk cow;
Old Bossy eats a bean;
Old Bossy is a crazy milk cow;
Color the other ear _____ (green).

Old Bossy is a crazy milk cow;
Old Bossy makes you think;
Old Bossy is a crazy milk cow;
Color her eyes _____ (pink).

Old Bossy is a crazy milk cow;
Old Bossy goes to bed;
Old Bossy is a crazy milk cow;
Color her cowbell _____ (red).

Old Bossy is a crazy milk cow;
Old Bossy just looks at you;
Old Bossy is a crazy milk cow;
Color her nose _____ (blue).

Old Bossy is a crazy milk cow;
Old Bossy goes to town;
Old Bossy is a crazy milk cow;
Color the rest of her _____ (brown).

Celebration of the Senses Day

If you can see it, hear it, smell it, taste it, or touch it,
you have your senses to thank.
So let's celebrate all of the senses with these fun activities.

Feel-Me Box

Find a medium-sized box, then turn it on its side and cut a hole large enough for a child's hand. Decorate the box as desired. Gather a large assortment of textured objects into a large opaque garbage bag. Include items such as a rock, sponge, pinecone, marble, small bag of ice, stuffed animal, etc. To play the game, place the box in front of you so that the open top of the box is now on the side and faces you while the hole for a child's hand is on the top. Discretely slip an item from the bag into the box so that the children cannot see it. Let a child reach into the box, to feel and describe the object inside. Repeat as time and interest allows.

Texture Trail

Remove shoes and socks. Line the children up and go for a walk through your class and outdoors feeling the different sensations with both your hands and feet. Does carpet feel different than concrete or sand? Do leaves feel different with your feet, hands, or face? Explore as many different textures in your environment as you can.

Spoon Repeat

Have the children sit at a table or hard floor. Give a spoon to each of the children and ask

them to hold the spoons in their laps while they listen to you tap. Tap a simple rhythm, such as three taps, and then invite the children to see if they can repeat it. Continue tapping rhythms as interest allows. Invite the children to tap rhythms for others to repeat.

Extension: Tap the rhythms of familiar songs, such as "Old MacDonald," to see if the children can correctly identify them.

Sound Cylinders

Fill two plastic eggs with identical small items. Secure the seams of the plastic eggs with tape. Make additional pairs by filling the eggs with pennies, rice, beans, flour, metal washers, small bells, water, etc. Let the children try to match the eggs that have the same contents by shaking and listening. How many pairs can be correctly identified? Have older children try to predict what makes the sound for each matching pair.

Variation: Fill many plastic eggs with rice to make shakers. Secure the eggs with narrow strips of duct tape. Play a recording of an appropriate song and let the children "shake" and move to the music.

Smelly Paints

Prepare two or three different pots of liquid tempera. Add several drops of strong food flavorings such as peppermint or lemon. Mix thoroughly and let the children create their own wonderful aromatic masterpieces at the easel.

Extension: Encourage the children to identify the flavorings or scents before beginning to paint.

Popcorn for the Senses

Make popcorn as a class and invite the children to see, hear, smell, touch, and taste the popcorn.

Extension: Talk about how popcorn pops (the moisture in the kernels turns to water vapor, expands, and explodes the kernel into the edible treat). Gather three different-sized containers. Measure ½ c. (118 ml) of popcorn and let the children observe the size of the kernels and compare the volume of the kernels in each of the three containers. After popping the popcorn, compare the volume of the popped corn to the kernels. To do this, first have the children predict which of the three containers they think the popcorn will fill. Pour the popped kernels into the smallest container first, and continue until you find a container large enough to hold all of the popcorn.

Food Favorites Tasting

Send home the parent/guardian note included at the end of this lesson, inviting the children in your class to bring small plates of finger food. Be sure there is enough of each item for every child to sample. Place the plates on a table. Next to each plate, tape to the table a copy of the Food Voting Chart (see page 60). Let the children taste one item from each plate and then vote by coloring in squares on the grids (depending on their tastes) on the Voting Charts. Once all children have had an opportunity to vote, count the colored squares to find out which food is the favorite.

Goofy Glasses

Copy the Goofy Glasses pattern page on heavy cardstock for each child. Let the children color and decorate their goofy glasses with markers and glitter. When finished, cut and assemble the glasses as shown on the pattern page. Wear your goofy glasses to see all sorts of imaginary and real wonders.

Extension: Have the children write stories while wearing their glasses. The stories can be compiled into a class book and enjoyed by all.

Dear Parents/Guardians,

On _____ we will be celebrating our senses and tasting different foods. Please help your child select a favorite finger food (such as fruits, vegetables, crackers, etc.) to share with the class. We will be tasting and voting to determine our class' favorite finger food!

Sincerely,

Food Voting Chart

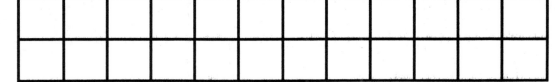

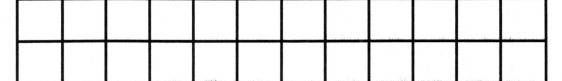

Cut out.

Cut out.

61

Blueberry Month

Did you know that some blueberries are actually black, that a blueberry can be as small as ¼ in. (6 mm) or as large as 1 in. (25 mm) in diameter and that blueberry bushes can grow to over 15 ft. (4.58 m) high? With these blueberry facts and fun activities, you'll never be content with plain old blueberry muffins again.

Blueberry Muffins

Have the children wash their hands and help you mix a batch of blueberry muffins from a mix or your favorite recipe. While you are waiting for the results, read the following storybook.

Story Time

Share the story *Blueberries for Sal* by Robert McClosky (Viking, 1948) with the children.

Extension: Play the game "Follow Me" and help "Sal" and "Little Bear" find their mothers. Divide the children into two groups and then separate them so that each group is on the opposite side of the room or playground. (Be sure to check that the area is free of obstacles.) Tell one group they are Sal's mother. Have them practice calling "Sal, Sal" in a high-pitched voice. Have the other group be "Mother Bear." Have that group pracice growling. Choose two children to be "It": one to be "Sal" and the other "Little Bear." Blindfold Sal and Little Bear and walk them to the middle of the playing area. Turn Sal and Little Bear around a few times to disorient them before beginning the game. At your signal, have the Mother Bear group and Sal's mother group begin calling their children. See who can find "Mother" in the shortest time by following the appropriate call home.

Kerplunk

You will need a tin can and a handful of marbles for this auditory discrimination activity. Have all the children put their heads down and close their eyes. Instruct them to listen carefully for the kerplink, kerplank, kerplunk sounds as you drop "blueberries" into the pail. See if the children can listen and correctly count the sound of each "blueberry" (marble) as it hits the bottom of the can. Have a child call out the number of blueberries. Repeat as interest and time allow.

Counting Blueberries

How many blueberries are there in one muffin? Before you eat all your blueberry muffins see if the children can guess how many blueberries there are in each muffin. Pull one muffin apart and separate all the blueberries. Place the berries in a line and count them. Invite the children to count the berries in their muffins (without pulling them apart) as they eat their muffins for snack.

Variation: Have the children work in pairs and count the blueberries in their muffins. Each pair reports their total. Which group has the most blueberries? the least?

Blue, Blue, and More Blue

Provide an assortment of blue media and collage materials for creating an absolutely blue picture. Suggestions might include: crayons, markers, paints, chalk, material scraps, colored paper, feathers, wallpaper, crepe paper—all in hues of blue.

Blueberry Dash

Cut several small "blueberries" (¾" [18 mm] circles) from dark blue construction paper (about 10 per child). Scatter the blueberries around the room or in an area outdoors. Give each child a small bag, then let the children see how many blueberries they can gather. Encourage the child who gathers the most to scatter all the blueberries again for a second blueberry dash. Repeat as interest and time allow.

Blueberry Pie

Make a copy of the Blueberry Pie pattern page for each child. Have the child color the pie crust and pan as desired. Thumbprint blueberries in the pie by stamping the thumb in a water-

soluble blue ink pad and then in the pie crust.

Variation: Make a "blueberry counting book" by writing a different math sentence on each copy of the Blueberry Pie pattern page. To complete each page, the children fingerprint the appropriate number of "berries" into the blueberry pie shell.

Painting with Blueberries

Freeze a small handful of blueberries. Place a piece of paper in the bottom of a 9" x 13" (23 x 33 cm) pan. Place two or three blueberries (or blue marbles) in a small bowl and cover completely with blue paint. Scoop the berries onto the paper in the pan, then move the pan from side to side to make a trail of paint as the blueberries roll back and forth over the paper.

Blueberry Muffins Dominoes

Make several copies of the Blueberry Muffin Dominoes pattern page on colored paper, mount on tagboard, and then cut apart the cards. Color the muffins as desired. Separate the cards and laminate them for durability. Play a lively game of "dominoes" by matching sets of blueberries on these yummy muffins. Shuffle the cards, then pass out the dominoes to the players. Leave one domino in the center of the playing area. Have the children take turns placing a domino in the playing area that matches one already played. The game continues until one player has no dominoes or until all dominoes have been played.

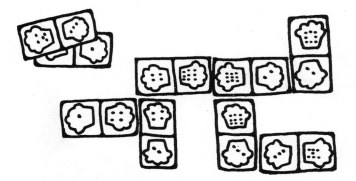

Coloring the Blues

Collect a sample recording of several different kinds of music such as classical, rock and roll, country-western, big band, rap, and of course "blues." Explain that music is written and performed to convey a message or feeling to the listener. Play a sampling of each type of music and see if the children can detect the differences in the music. Note the different tempos, beats, and dynamics of the pieces you have selected. Encourage the children to relate how the "blues" music makes them feel. Provide each child with a piece of paper and a blue crayon. Have the children draw "pictures" (anything from scribbles to concrete objects) of the music as you play the "blues" for them.

Extension: Discuss the different instruments that are played in the various pieces of music. Can the children pick out the drums, the horns, or strings? If possible, show pictures of the instruments. Make your own "blues" music with classroom instruments or various objects turned into musical instruments.

Berry Trails

Using a water-soluble blue ink pad, have each child fingerprint "berries" on paper. When the child is finished, see how many of the "berries" can be connected by drawing lines between them. Can you create pictures or shapes of objects by connecting the berries?

Variation: Have each child print 20 "berries" on a paper. Then randomly number the berries 1–20. (The numbers do not necessarily have to be placed in order just as long as every number is used on the page.) Trade papers with a friend and see if you can connect the dots in order from 1 to 20 to make a crazy blue web dot-to-dot picture.

Blueberry Pie

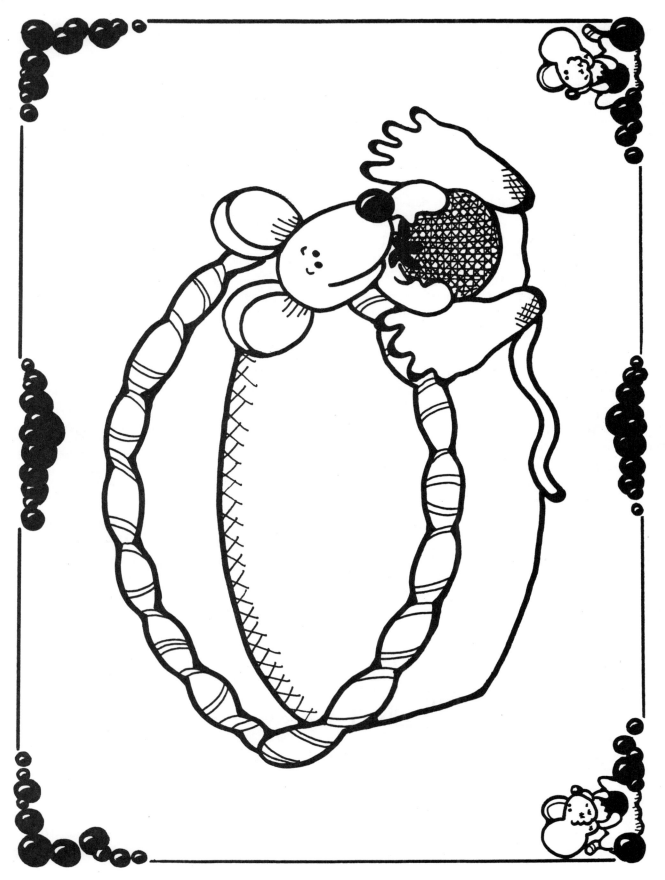

National Ice Cream Day

Americans consume an average of 15 quarts of ice cream per person each year.
Consume your share of fun with these ice cream activities.

Wiggle and Freeze

Ice cream is made from a liquid mixture which is frozen by applying ice. Have the children wiggle their bodies as though they are made of liquid until you say "freeze." They must stop in whatever positions their bodies are in and wait for your next direction. Next, tell the children to "melt" until they form a "puddle" on the floor. Continue freezing and melting as time and interest allow.

Scoops

Mix a large batch of instant potatoes to a firm consistency. (If interested, color the potatoes by adding food coloring to the milk before adding the flakes.) Provide a few empty ice cream cones and a couple of ice cream scoops and let the children try scooping ice cream that never melts.

Variation: Set up the materials along with play money and a toy cash register in the dramatic play area for your budding entrepreneurs.

Ice Cream Scoop Count

Provide several sheets of colored paper, circle stencils (such as small plastic lids from potato chip containers), and scissors. Then have the children trace and cut out circles. (If appropriate, precut the circles for the children). Make a copy of the Ice Cream Sundae dish on page 68 for each child. After pasting the "ice cream" circles inside the sundae dish, have the child count the

total number of scoops shown and write the number on the dish.

Variation: For delicious "ice cream" math facts, make several copies of pattern page 68. Write math sentences on the cones or ice cream dishes for the children to finish, such as "3 + 6 = ___." Color and cut out the shapes, mounting them on construction paper. Have the child add the appropriate number of "scoops of ice cream" to the cone or dish to complete the math sentence.

Ice Cream Hide and Seek

Use an empty ice cream cone for ice cream hide and seek. Have one child leave the room while another child hides the cone. Remind the children that where the cone is hidden is "a secret" and that the only clues you can give is by the loudness of your voice. Invite the child back into the room and have the class quietly chant, "I scream, you scream, we all scream for ice cream" over and over again, getting gradually louder as the child approaches the hidden cone. When the child finds the cone, have her choose the next child to hide the cone. Repeat the game as many times as possible.

Will It Freeze?

Have the children investigate what happens to the liquids when placed in a freezer. Pour a small amount of the ice cream mix (see recipe on page 67) in an ice cube tray. Fill a few cavities in the tray with water. Prepare a second tray by filling some cavities with water and others with ice cream mix. Place this tray in the refrigerator. Every hour observe the trays and compare the results. Record the children's observations on chart paper.

66

Ice-Melting Experiments

Freeze two trays each of ice cubes made of red, yellow, and blue colored water to create colored ice. Place two differently colored cubes in a bowl and let the children predict what color the water will be when the two ice cubes melt. Let the children hypothesize and investigate ways to make the ice melt faster (e.g., adding water to the ice, placing the pan in a warm place, etc.).

Variation: What can you do to prevent the ice cubes from melting? Have the children investigate ways to insulate their ice cubes and then measure to find out which ice cube stayed frozen the longest. Give each team a colored ice cube in a resealable plastic bag. Have the students use various materials to insulate their ice cubes. This is an ideal time to investigate how effective different picnic coolers are.

Ice Cream Survey

Make a graph listing different ice cream flavors for each column. Survey the class and graph the results of the favorite flavors. If there were no more vanilla ice cream, how many children would be disappointed?

Variation: Have each child take a survey sheet home to ask family members about their favorite ice cream flavors. Tally the results in the classroom.

King or Queen of Ice Cream

When ice cream was first invented, there were no freezers to keep it frozen. As a result, only kings and queens could afford to have ice cream. Create and decorate the front of a crown as desired on construction paper, then cut it out. Cut a strip of construction paper in thirds lengthwise. Staple one end of the strip to either side of the crown. Wear your crown while you feast on ice cream and feel like a king or queen for the day.

Variation: Write a story about a king/queen and ice cream. Use a copy of page 69 as a cover for the book. Be sure to write the title on the cover.

Homemade Ice Cream

To make your own ice cream, use an ice cream freezer, or you can make your own ice cream freezer by using two metal cans. Use a large #10 metal coffee can and a second can of a smaller size. Fill the smaller can with the ice cream mixture. Seal the smaller can with a tight lid, then secure the lid with duct tape. Place the smaller can inside the larger can and pack crushed ice, a little water, and ½ c. (118 ml) rock salt around the smaller can. Seal the outer container with a lid. Let the children shake and roll the ice cream inside the can for 15 minutes. Open, stir the ice cream, and repack as directed above. Continue rolling and shaking for another 5–10 minutes or until the ice cream mixture hardens.

Basic Ice Cream

1 c. (237 ml) sugar
1 c. (240 ml) scalded milk
Dash of salt
1 c. (240 ml) half and half cream
1½ tsp. (7.5 ml) vanilla extract
2 c. (480 ml) heavy whipping cream

To flavor your ice cream, add 2 cups (474 ml) of your favorite fruit. Chill the mixture for 30 minutes before pouring it into your ice cream freezer.

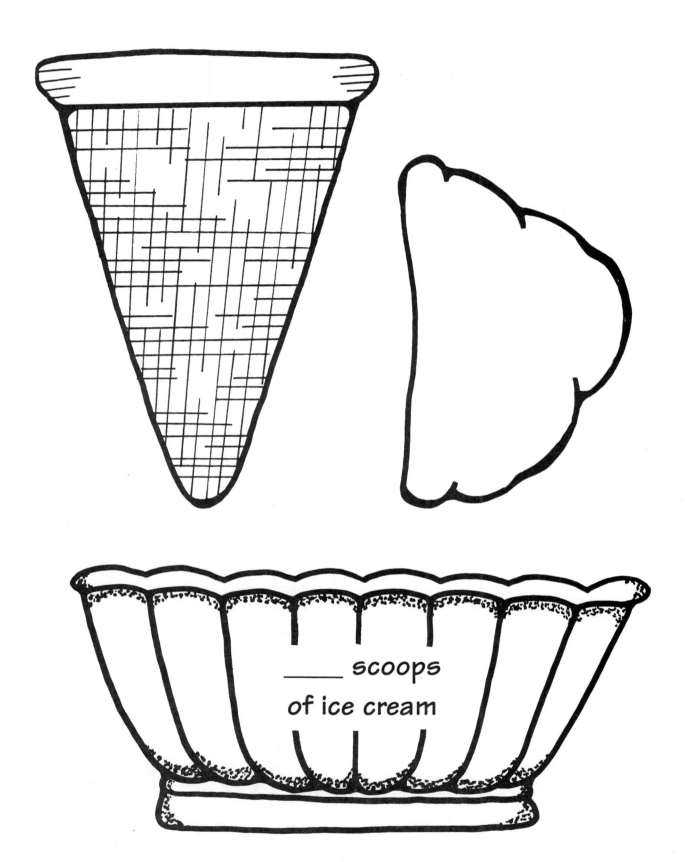

_____ scoops
of ice cream

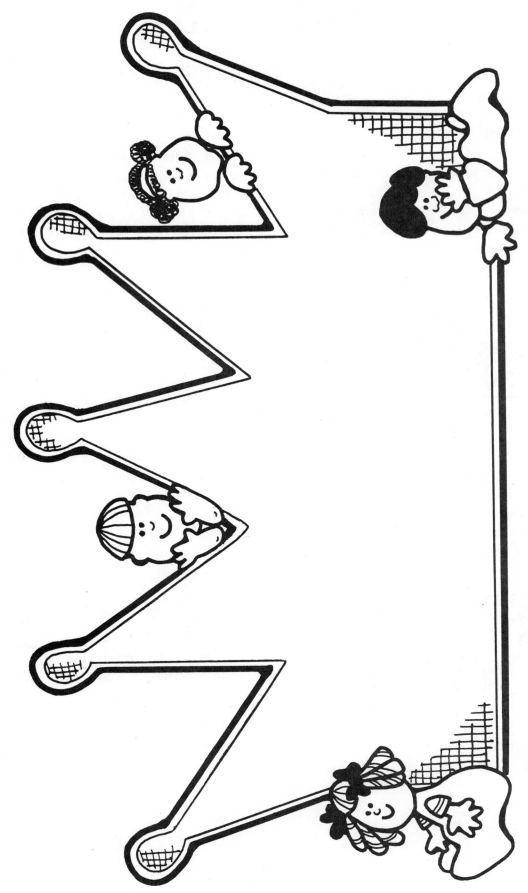

IF01366 Holidays for Dull Days

Mustard Day

*Mustard has gained its fame as a spicy sandwich spread.
Spread your own fun with these Mustard Day activities.*

Mustard Painting

Twist the top of a squeezable mustard container so that a thin line of mustard flows easily from the bottle. Give the children construction paper and let them create their own mustard art by drawing with the mustard bottle. What happens when the mustard dries?

Dry Mustard Art

Use a glue stick or paste to rub designs on a piece of paper. Sprinkle dry mustard spice over the paper and shake to cover all the glue. Stand the paper on its side and tap excess powder from the paper to create mustard art of a different kind. When finished, examine the mustard with magnifying glasses. Have the children share their observations.

Making Mustard Topping

Compare powdered mustard to mustard in a jar. What would you need to add to the dry mustard spice to create the gelatin substance that you squeeze on sandwiches? Read the ingredient list on the bottle and see if you can create your own mustard.

Mustard Tracks

Tape one end of a skein of yellow yarn to the floor. Continue making yellow "mustard tracks" by stretching the yarn around the room and taping it to the floor in strategic places. Let the children walk along the mustard tracks heel to toe and then again backwards without falling off the line.

Variations: Create four or five different tracks. Be sure to crisscross the yarn lines. When finished, place a mustard bottle at the end of one of the tracks. Have the children walk along the string tracks trying to discover which path leads to the mustard bottle.

Cut three or four different lengths of string, then tape a different colored paper to the end of each string. Create tracks as indicated above. Have the children see if they can determine visually which string path is the longest. Record their predictions by writing their names on the corresponding pieces of colored paper. Have the children check their predictions by counting their footsteps from one end of each string to the other.

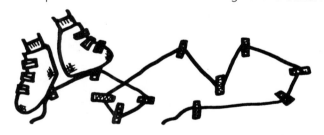

Mustard Color Match

What other objects can you find that match the color of mustard? Send your children on a scavenger hunt around the room to find other objects that are yellow.

Variation: Have the children clip pictures from magazines that match the color of mustard. Use the pictures to create a mustard-colored collage or have the children use the pictures in a story about mustard.

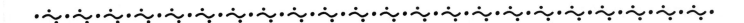

The Mustard on My Sandwich
Action Rhyme

With the children standing arms' lengths apart, read the rhyme shown below and perform the corresponding actions. If interested, add to the rhyme by finding new body parts and actions.

Variation: Write the rhyme on sentence strips. If appropriate, talk about the words that rhyme, blends, or initial consonant sounds. Circle the words or word parts on the sentence strips at the appropriate times.

The Mustard on My Sandwich
Goes Plop, Plop, Plop!

My toes inside my shoes go tap, tap, tap.
  (Tap toes.)
My hands on my knees go slap, slap, slap.
  (Slap knees.)
My feet on the floor go hop, hop, hop.
  (Hop on one foot.)
While the mustard on my sandwich goes plop,
  plop, plop! (Pound hand with fist.)

My bones when it's cold go shake, shake, shake.
  (Shake body.)
My tongue likes to "hiss" like a snake, snake,
  snake. (Move arms like a snake as you hiss.)
My hands pat my head on top, top, top.
  (Pat head.)
While the mustard on my sandwich goes plop,
  plop, plop! (Pound hand with fist.)

My head when it's sleepy likes to nod, nod, nod.
  (Nod head.)
My mouth when I yawn looks rather odd, odd,
  odd. (Stretch arms and yawn.)
My hips when I'm dancing go bop, bop, bop.
  (Move hips side to side.)
While the mustard on my sandwich goes plop,
  plop, plop! (Pound hand with fist.)

Pass the Mustard

While holding a bottle of mustard, begin a story about a little bottle of mustard. Pass the mustard bottle to a child in your class and have him continue the story. That child then passes the mustard to another child. When she is finished, she passes the mustard bottle to a different child. The story is continued until everyone in the class has an opportunity to add to the mustard story.

Hot Mustard Game

Have the children sit in a circle. Give each child a paper plate. Ask one child to be "It" and to turn himself around, facing the outside of the circle and covering his eyes. Play the "hot mustard" game by passing a squeezable mustard container around the circle. When the child who is "It" calls "Stop," the child who is caught with the mustard bottle in her hands must squeeze a dollop of mustard on her plate. This person then becomes "It" and the game continues. The winner is determined by the person with the fewest spots of mustard on the plate at the end of the game.

Mustard Match

Make two copies of the Mustard Match pattern on heavy cardstock. Color the mustard bottles as desired. Laminate for durability. For this matching activity the child places the bottles with identical shapes next to one another.

Variations: Arrange the bottles *face down* for a memory match game. Have each child take a turn to find the matching pairs. The child keeps the mustard bottles if the match is correct. If the bottles do not match, place the bottles face down again and the next player takes a turn. For other memory match games make matching pairs of mustard bottles for practicing consonant sounds, rhyming pictures, letters of the alphabet, math facts, etc.

Mustard Squish

Make a copy of the mustard bottle pattern for each child. Cut out the shape on the solid black line around the outside edge. Fold the pattern in half along the dotted line. Place a dollop of mustard inside the folded piece of paper. Lay the paper flat on a table while pounding and rubbing the outside of the paper. Open to reveal an interesting mustard design.

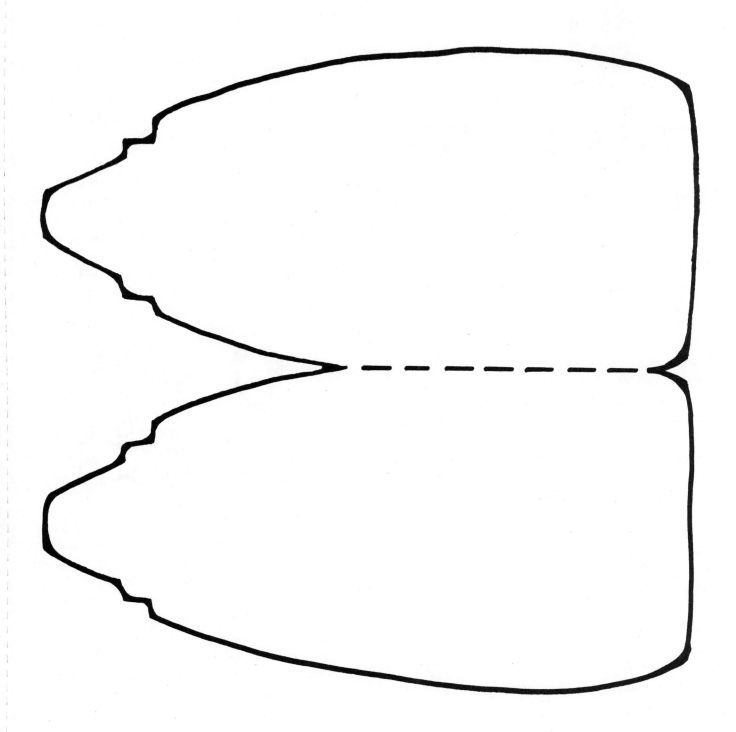

Mosquito Awareness Day

*A mosquito's wings beat 1,000 times a second.
You'll have to move faster than that to keep up with all the fun planned for this celebration.*

Bug Swatter Art

This project can be quite messy and should be done outdoors. Place sheets of newspaper down on the sidewalk. Place a large sheet of paper on top of the newspaper. Fill two or three pans with tempera paint, each a different color. Dip a bug swatter in the paint and then slap it down on the paper (provide a separate bug swatter for each color of paint). Repeat using other colors as desired. Be sure the young artists are wearing paint smocks!

Proboscis Practice

Cut several small squares of scrap paper, then spread them on a table. Place an empty bowl or pan at the opposite end of the table. Provide a straw for each child. Let each child try to use his/her "proboscis" by sucking through a straw to pick up pieces of paper and deposit them into the bowl at the end of the table.

Variations: Place several bowls on the opposite end of the table. Label each bowl with a different number. Have the children fill the bowls with the corresponding number of paper squares to work on number recognition.

Have the children work with partners. One team member uses a timer or watch with a second hand to time the other team member. The partner is given one minute to collect pieces of paper with the "proboscis." Record the total and trade responsibilities.

Mosquito Exploration

Encourage the children to explore more about mosquitoes. For instance, find out what animals eat mosquitoes and what do mosquitoes eat. If possible, provide books for the children to "read" as they find out more about mosquitoes.

Buzz Session

Decorate the outside of a cardboard tube. Cover one end with a small square of waxed paper and secure it with a rubber band. When each child has made the sound maker, have a "Mosquito Buzz Session" by humming into the tubes.

Variation: See if you can create or find other musical instruments that vibrate to make sound (e.g., kazoos, drums, strings). Be sure to observe how the sounds are made.

Story Time

Locate a copy of the African folktale *Why Mosquitoes Buzz in People's Ears* (Dial Press, 1975) to read to the children. When the children are familiar with the book, retell the story by having the children perform the different animal parts.

Variation: Start your own mosquito buzz game by having the children sit in a circle. Whisper a phrase into the ear of the child on your left. He then whispers what he heard to the child on his left, who whispers the phrase to the next child and so on around the circle. The last child in the circle then repeats what she heard aloud. It is surprising how much a "mosquito's buzz" can change.

Musical Mosquitoes

Female mosquitoes buzz in higher tones than male mosquitoes (the wings make the sound). For this activity the children can buzz "high" and "low." First, prepare a Musical Mosquitoes Singing Stick by copying the pattern on heavy cardstock or construction paper. Color the mosquitoes and cut them out. Tape a dowel or straw to the backside of one of the mosquitoes. Tape the other mosquito on top of the first mosquito and dowel so that both faces can be seen.

Choose a favorite song to sing as a class. When Ms. Mosquito is facing the children, they should sing the song as high as they can. When Mr. Mosquito is turned to face the children, they should lower the pitch of the song and sing as low as they can. Let the children each take turns directing the class with the singing stick, seeing if the rest of the class can follow their directions.

Scratch Tag

Play a game of scratch tag by choosing one child to be the "mosquito." All the other children should try to avoid the mosquito. If "bitten" (tagged) by the mosquito, they must then scratch the spot where the mosquito tagged them as they continue running to avoid being bitten again. The first person to receive two bites becomes the next mosquito.

Ouch! Mosquito Bites

Provide a copy of the pattern on page 78 for each child to decorate (color the skin, add hair and clothes, as desired). For this "Ouch" game, have the children work in pairs. Each player takes a turn at spinning the dial (see Sock-It-to-Me on page 44 for instructions) and then stamps the corresponding number of "mosquito bites" on the body figure. To create the "bites" use a red stamp pad (water-soluble ink) and a pencil eraser. When the first player reaches 10 bites, the game ends. The other player is the winner because no one wants mosquito bites. If interested, have the players wear their mosquito headbands (see page 79) when playing the game.

Variations: Provide decorated and laminated copies of the game board. Have the players use red markers to make the "mosquito bites." When the game ends, use a damp cloth to erase the bites. Play again as time and interest allow.

Have the entire class play the game at the same time. When finished count all the bites and arrive at a class total. Which team has the most "bites"? the fewest?

Mosquito Slap Game

Prepare the Mosquito Slap Game cards by making eight copies of the pattern page on heavy cardstock. Color and cut out the cards. Laminate them for durability, if desired.

To play: Begin the game when two or four players want to play. Deal all of the cards face down to the players. Have a child begin by placing the card on top of his pile *face up* in the middle of the game area. If the card depicts a "male" mosquito, play continues to the left. The next child turns a card *face up* in the center of the playing area. If a "female" mosquito card is played, the players try to be the first to slap the "female mosquito" picture card (since she's the one who will bite you because she needs blood for the babies) by slapping their hands down on the cards in the middle of the players. The first player to slap the "female" mosquito collects the discarded cards in the middle, turns them *face down* and adds them to the bottom of her card pile. Play resumes to the left. The game ends when only one player has cards and is declared the winner.

Variation: Prepare several copies of the cards and have the students use them to create patterns: ABAB, ABBA, AABB, etc.

Mosquito Slap Game

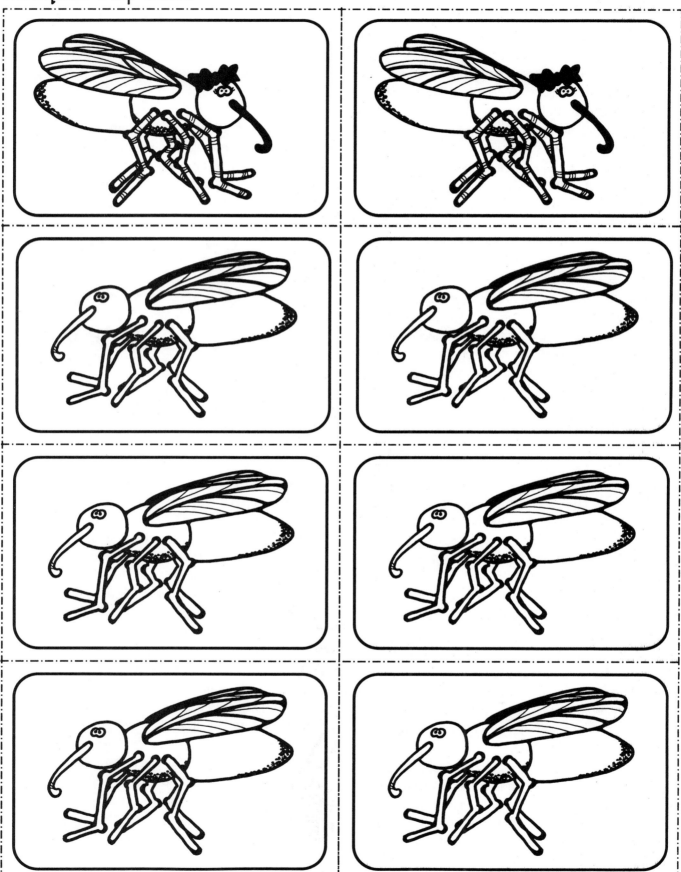

IF01366 Holidays for Dull Days

Ouch! Mosquito Bites!

No Bites!

No Bites!

Mosquito Headband

Make one copy for each child on heavy cardstock. Color and cut out the mosquito. Cut a second sheet of paper in thirds lengthwise and staple one length to either end of the mosquito to create a headband. To make the "proboscis" for each mosquito headband, cut ½" (13 mm) strips of black construction paper. Curl the strip of black construction paper by rolling it around a pencil. Paste one end of the "proboscis" below the eyes on the headband to complete the project.

Honey Month

*Bees make this high-energy food by combining nectar and special enzymes.
After celebrating this holiday, you'll be stuck on honey, too!*

Honeybee Exploration

Encourage the children to learn more about honeybees. Provide books for the children to "read" by looking at the pictures. Talk about the bee's body, the different members in a hive, how pollen and nectar are collected by the honeybees, and the stages of the honeybee's life cycle. If possible, invite a beekeeper to visit your classroom and show a real honeycomb as well as some of the tools that are used to collect the honey.

Hickety-Tickety Honeybee

Prepare the honeybee wand on pattern page 82. Make a copy of the pattern on heavy cardstock paper, then color it as desired. Cut out the honeybee shape and laminate it for durability. Secure the honeybee to the top of a dowel with masking tape.

Invite the children to sit in a circle. As you point to a child with the honeybee wand, say the following poem:

Hickety-tickety honeybee
Please say your name for me.

After a child responds correctly to the request, the person holding the wand should respond with a "thank-you" before moving to another child.

Variation: In place of "Please say your name for me," substitute other requests: naming words that begin with certain letters or blends, words that rhyme, identifying colors by naming objects, reading word cards, practicing math facts, stating numbers that are greater or less than a number, stating a number one less or two less than a specified number, counting backwards from a specified number, or counting by 5s, 10s, 20s. Request cards can be prepared beforehand for the children to use when holding the honeybee wand. The child who answers the request correctly gets to hold the wand and make a request for a different player.

Nectar Game

Make several copies of the Nectar Game pattern pieces on heavy cardstock so that there are at least four flowers and four nectar drops for each player. Color the flowers, then cut out and laminate all pieces for durability. Place a nectar drop (roll a piece of tape and place it on the back of each) on each flower, before taping the flowers around the room.

Before beginning the game, explain to the players that in order to make honey, worker bees must first gather nectar from flowers. The bees put the nectar in special pouches on their legs and then fly back to the beehive and deposit the nectar in special six-sided wax cups called a honeycomb.

Prepare the honeycomb first by having the children help you fit all the wax cups (six-sided shapes) together and tape them to the floor to complete the honeycomb puzzle.

At your signal, the children while wearing their honeybee headband (see page 86) fly off to find nectar to bring back to the hive. Have the children pull the nectar drops off the flowers and stick them to their legs (they'll need their wings for the return flight). Once back at the beehive, the children should place their nectar drops in empty sections of the honeycomb and then leave to find other flowers. Continue playing until all the nectar has been collected and placed in the honeycomb cups.

Variation: Use yellow pattern blocks (hexagon shape) to create honeycombs. If appropriate, have the children explore how many hexagon shapes they would need as a class to create a honeycomb (e.g., having 5, 8, or 11 partitions) for each student. Use math counters to arrive at a class total.

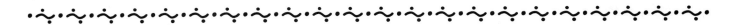

Honey Butter

½ c. (118 ml) butter or margarine
¾ c. (180 ml) honey
Dash of vanilla flavoring

Whip the mixture. To serve, spread on a slice of warm bread. Keep chilled in the refrigerator when not in use.

Sticky Bees

Make a copy of the Sticky Bees activity page for each child. Have each child color and cut out the bees and beehive. (You may wish to draw a line around each bee for the child to follow when cutting out the bees.) Paste the beehive on another sheet of colored construction paper. Stick each bee on or near the hive with a small dot of honey applied with a cotton swab. Have the child count the bees when finished and write the number on the paper. *Extension:* Write a number on a card for each child. The child then glues the corresponding number of bees on his hive.

Variation: Create file folder games that work on addition or subtraction facts. Color the hive and paste it on one side of the folder. Have a few bees flying around the hive by gluing some to the file folder. Write math facts on index cards. Make 20 bees as game pieces, then laminate them and the hive for durability. Place two rough Velcro strips on the hive and small fuzzy Velcro pieces on the backs of the bees. Let the children take turns drawing a fact card and placing the corresponding number of bees on the Velcro strips as indicated by the math equation. If adding, have the child count the subsets and arrive at the sum. If subtracting, have the child complete the steps to find the difference. Of course, the child may wish to wear her honeybee headband during the activity. Each time the answer is correct, the child collects a nectar drop (see page 83 for pattern). At the end of a predetermined time, you may wish to have the players turn in 5 or 10 nectar drops for a prize.

Stuck in the Honey Game

Give one child the honeybee wand (see Hickety-Tickety Honeybee for wand directions) and have her stand outside the circle of children. The child who is "It" then walks around the outside of the circle. While chanting, "I had a little bee and he won't sting you," she GENTLY taps each child in turn on the head. At some point, the child who is "It" selects another child to be "It" by saying, "But he will sting YOU!" The child who is "It" then drops the wand into the selected child's lap and races around the outside of the circle back to the spot where the second child had been seated. At the same time, the second child jumps up and chases after "It," trying to catch "It" before "It" runs all the way around the circle. If the second child does catch "It," the child who was "It" must sit in the sticky honey pot (in the middle of the circle of children) and watch as the game continues with the second child now playing "It."

Bee Finger Puppets

Make copies of the pattern page for the children. Color as desired, cut out and assemble the bees to make some buzzing finger fun.

Extension: Have the children work with partners and create stories or finger plays about the honeybees. Encourage the children to perform their work for other classmates.

IF01366 Holidays for Dull Days

Nectar Game

IF01366 Holidays for Dull Days

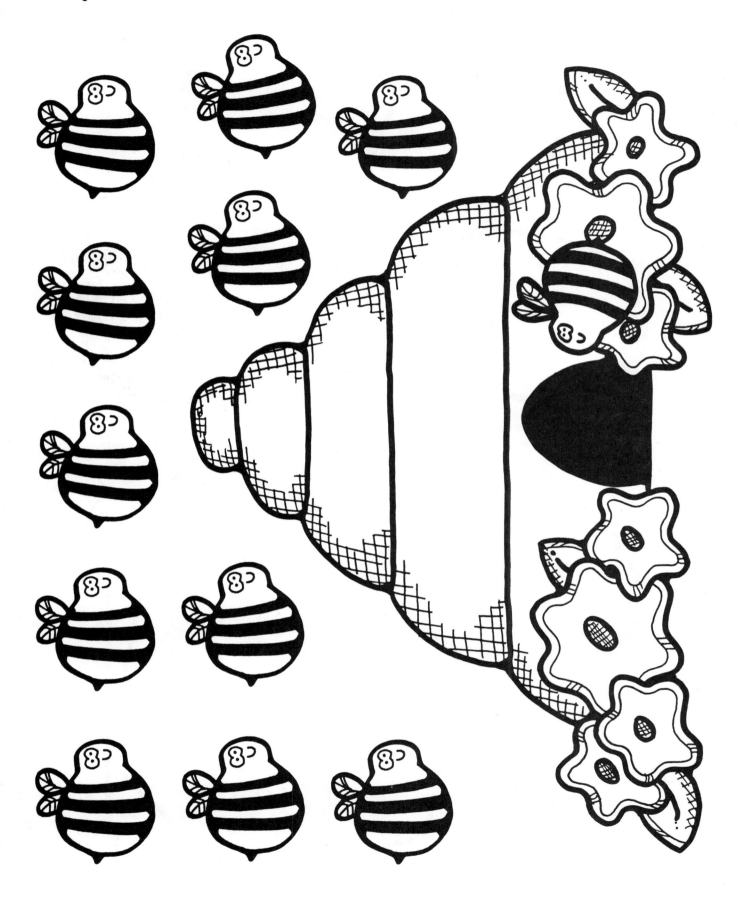

IF01366 *Holidays for Dull Days*

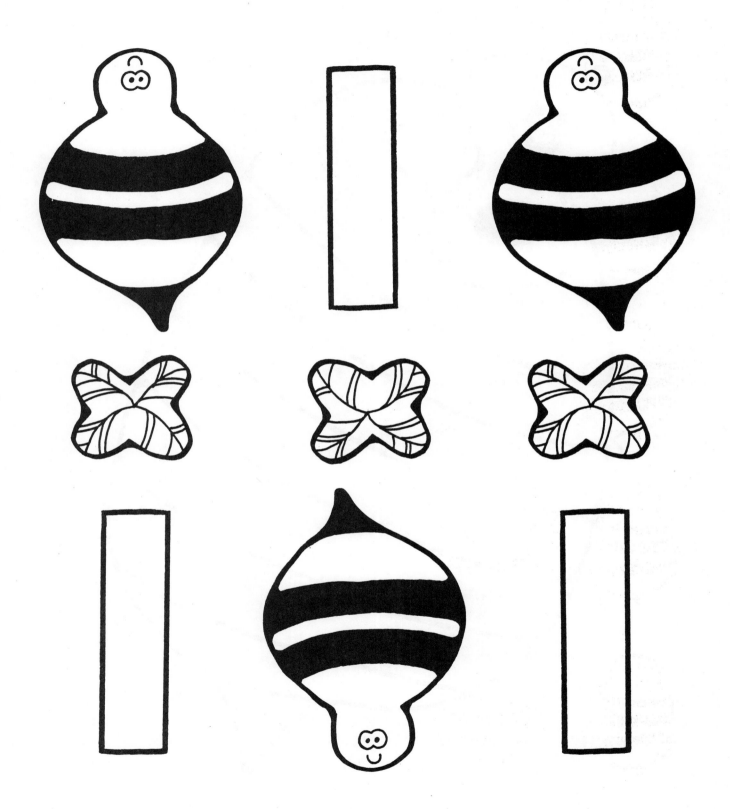

Honeybee Headband

Make one copy for each child on heavy cardstock. Color as desired, then cut it out. Cut a large circle (approximately 10" [25 cm] in diameter) from yellow tissue paper. Gather the circle through the middle and glue to the small "x" on the back of the honeybee to create its wings. Cut a second sheet of paper in thirds lengthwise and staple one length to either end of the bee to create a headband.

Elephant Appreciation Day

Did you know that the largest land mammal, the elephant, sleeps standing up?
Your class will not want to sleep through any of this day of elephant fun.

Elephant Exploration

Encourage the children to learn more about elephants. Provide books for the children to "read" by looking at the pictures. Talk about the elephant's body, where elephants live, how African and Asian elephants differ, and the foods elephants eat. If possible, watch a video tape about elephants.

Peanut Drop

Place a tin can on the floor behind a chair. Kneel on the chair facing its back and hold a peanut on your nose. Leaning slightly over the back of the chair, see if you can drop the peanut into the can.

Variations: Arrange two chairs and cans instead of one set. Write numbers on the peanuts. Have the children read the numbers and then try to drop even numbered peanuts into one can and odd numbers into the other can. Be sure the children do not eat any of the numbered peanuts.

Working in a small group with two or three children, have the team estimate how many peanuts they think the team can drop into the bucket if each player is given five tries. Have one student tally the results as the peanuts are dropped. Encourage the children to compare their results with their estimates.

Elephant Train

For a train of elephants, have the children line up in a straight line, one in front of the other. then each child reaches one hand in front of him/her as the "trunk" and stretches back with the other hand as the "tail." Finish the elephant train by having the children grab the elephant's tail in front of them with their trunks. Parade around the room, swinging tails and trunks as you go.

Variation: Have all the children stand still in the elephant train. Let the lead elephant start a chain reaction by squeezing the hand of the child behind her. The next child in turn squeezes the hand of the child behind him until the hand squeeze reaches the end of the train. When the end "elephant" receives a squeeze he or she moves to the front of the line and starts the chain reaction over again. (You may wish to divide the class into smaller teams and play this activity as a relay game.)

"Mellow" Elephants

Begin by sticking four miniature marshmallows each on five toothpicks leaving 1/2" (13 mm) of the toothpick exposed to create four legs and a trunk. With scissors, cut a large marshmallow in thirds to create ears. Stick two of these ear slices on either side of a large marshmallow and secure by poking a toothpick through the ears and head. Stick the head to another large marshmallow for the body and secure it with a toothpick. Stick the four legs into the bottom of the elephant body. Then stick the trunk to the head in between the ears to create your "mellow" elephant.

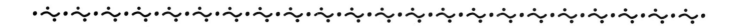

Elephant Trunks

Request parent donations of laundered nylon stockings for this activity. Cut the pantyhose off at the legs. Let each child wad balls of newspaper and fill the stocking from toe to top. Tie a string on either side of the stocking and then tie it around the child's face to make an elephant's trunk. Have fun acting like an elephant.

Mouse and Elephant Tag

Legend has it that elephants are afraid of mice. Prepare the Mouse Necklace (see page 91) by copying the pattern on heavy cardstock. Color and cut out the mouse. Laminate the picture for durability. Punch holes where indicated with small dots. Cut a 24" (61 cm) length of yarn and attach it to the mouse through the holes to create a necklace.

To play the game, designate a corner of the play area as a "jungle." Choose one child to be "It." This child should wear the mouse necklace. "It" attempts to catch the elephants by tagging them and then takes them back to the jungle. Once all the elephants have been caught, choose a new mouse and play again.

The Story of Five Huge Elephants

Prepare the pictures provided to illustrate the Five Huge Elephants flannel board story printed below. Copy the elephants on heavy cardstock, then color them as desired and cut them out. Attach felt or flannel to the back of the illustrations. Using the pictures, share the rhyme with the children. As each stanza is finished, have the children complete the phrase with the appropriate number.

Variation: Instead of making a flannel board story, make the pictures into cards, or have the children act out the parts of the elephants while wearing their "elephant trunks." Add more numbers (6–10) to the poem, creating your own rhymes.

Five Huge Elephants

Five huge elephants marching out the door,
One stopped to read a book and then there were _____. (four).
Four huge elephants standing by a tree,
One fell asleep standing up and then there were _____. (three)
Three huge elephants trying on some shoes,
One stopped to tie a knot and then there were _____. (two)
Two huge elephants playing in the sun,
One jumped into a pool and then there was _____. (one)
One huge elephant sitting all alone,
He drove off to find his friends and then there were _____. (none)

Counting Elephants

Make two copies of the picture cards on page 92 for each team of children. Color and cut apart the cards, then laminate them for durability. For a memory match game, follow the instructions on page 31 (Noodle Matching Game).

Variations: If appropriate, give the child two or three cards and encourage him to write a math sentence using the numbers shown. For example: "2 + 3 + 4 = ____." Provide lots of peanuts as counters to help the child solve the math problem.

Mouse Necklace

Me Week

We all have similarities and differences which make each of us unique and important.
This is a week to celebrate the fact that you are the only one exactly like you! (This unit can be celebrated at any
time of the year or in conjunction with Universal Children's Week during the first week of October.)

Match Me

A few days before beginning this activity, send a letter home to parents/guardians (see letter at the end of this lesson) requesting a current picture and photograph of each child as an infant. Make a copy of each photograph and mount it on construction paper. Color as desired and laminate for durability.

Display all of the pictures in a special area. Let the children try to match each child's baby picture to the correct current picture. Once all the children's pictures have been correctly identified, write the child's name on each of the photos and use the cards for a memory matching game.

"All About Me!" Bags

Have each child collect 10 items from home that represent him/herself, such as photographs, mementos, or possessions that indicate likes or preferences. Place all items in a brown paper bag and decorate the bag as desired. (See parent letter at the end of this lesson).

Give each child the opportunity to share his/her bag with the group by showing and explaining its contents. Have other children listen for differences or similarities of all the children's bags. Talk about how no two bags are exactly alike—just as no two children are exactly alike.

Graphing Similarities/Differences

Draw a set of squares to form a graph on a large sheet of paper, or you may use the graph provided on page 97. Talk about the things that are similar among the children (e.g., We all have two eyes) and the things that are different (e.g., Our eye colors can be different from one another). Record the similarities and differences on the graph. Let each child color in the squares that correspond to him/her. For instance, a child who has brown hair should color in the first square next to where brown hair is listed on the graph. When finished, discuss the results shown on the graph.

Me! Puzzles

Take a picture of each child (or request a photograph be brought from home). Enlarge the photograph to 8½" x 11" (216 x 279 mm) by copying the picture and then mount it on construction paper.

Have the children color the photos of themselves using watercolor markers or pastels. If appropriate, let the children draw a puzzle design on the back of the picture and then cut out the pieces. You may want to cut the page into shapes for younger children. Place the pieces of each puzzle in an envelope so that each child has a puzzle of him/herself to assemble over and over again!

Thumbs Up/Thumbs Down

Use the list of characteristics provided on page 96 or make a list of a minimum of 10–15 favorites (you can list as many as time and interest will allow) such as colors, television shows, foods, or life experiences (e.g., moving to a new house, losing a tooth). Perhaps the children would like to brainstorm ideas for the list.

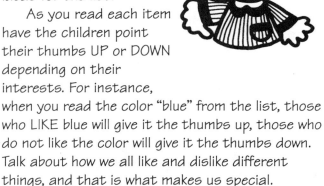

As you read each item have the children point their thumbs UP or DOWN depending on their interests. For instance, when you read the color "blue" from the list, those who LIKE blue will give it the thumbs up, those who do not like the color will give it the thumbs down. Talk about how we all like and dislike different things, and that is what makes us special.

Variations: As you read the items on the list, have the children predict how many of the children will respond with a "thumbs up" for each question. Record your predictions on the chalkboard. Tally the responses to the questions as the children make the thumbs up sign. Compare the responses to the predictions.

Give each child a copy of the Thumbs Up/Thumbs Down activity sheet. Encourage each child to find another classmate that matches each description given (e.g., Find someone who has lost two teeth). The child should then write the name of the student next to the description and move to another child to find a match to another question.

Write notes to the children listing the things you feel are important or special about them. Be sure to include how each child is an important addition to your class!

Guess Who?

A few days before beginning this activity, send a letter home to parents/guardians (see letter at the end of this lesson) requesting that they write down five things that make their child special. With your class, read items from the collected information and see if the children can guess which child you are describing.

Me! Banners

Make a copy of the activity sheet on page 98 for each child. (You may wish to draw a line around each bear before copying the sheet. This makes it easier for the children to cut out the bears.) To make a banner, cut a sheet of construction paper in half lengthwise and tape the pieces together at the short ends for the child. Have the child trace his hands onto the banner and then write his name. Let the child add details by cutting out the head shape on the pattern page, drawing features and hair to make it into a self-portrait, and then gluing it on the banner. Next, give the child an opportunity to choose a few pictures representing his/her "likes" from the pattern page (or clip magazine pictures) to add to the banner. Color, cut out, and paste the chosen bears to the banner. (When the girls make their banners, they may decorate the bears to make them appear as girls also.) Tape or glue a stick or straw to the end of each banner and have a parade!

Variation: If appropriate, have the children clip words or phrases out of magazines or newspapers that describe themselves to add to their banners.

"My Child Is Special . . ." Activity

Dear Parents/Guardians,

Next week we will be celebrating how each child is different. Please write down five things that make your child special, and return this page to me by _____. Be as specific as possible, and try to include one story about something funny or unusual your child has said or done in the past, something that will not embarrass your child. We will read each idea and guess who it is about!

1.

2.

3.

4.

5.

Sincerely,

"All About Me Bag!" Activity

Dear Parents/Guardians,

While celebrating "Me Week" we will learn about one another in our class and what is important to each of us. Please send an "All About Me!" bag (see instructions below) with your child on _____. We will be showing them during our group time on this day.

To create an "All About Me!" bag, find a large brown paper bag to collect memorabilia or other representations of the important things in your child's life. Have your child decorate the outside of the bag. Place items or pictures inside the bag that characterize your child's favorite colors and foods, hobbies, family, pets, and special trips or awards. Be sure to plan ahead as the fun of this project comes in doing it TOGETHER!

Sincerely,

Photograph Request Letter

Dear Parents/Guardians,

To celebrate "Me Week" we will be talking about the importance of each child in our group. We need your help! Will you please provide:

* a photograph of your child as an infant

* a current photograph of your child.

I will need these items by _____. I will be making photocopies of the photographs for use in some fun projects and will take great care in returning these precious memories to you.

Sincerely,

Thumbs Up/Thumbs Down

 • Find someone with a ribbon or barrettes in her hair.

 • Find someone who is missing some teeth.

 • Find someone with a number on the clothes.

 • Find someone who has a pet at home.

 • Find someone who likes the same color as you.

 • Find someone who is wearing colored socks (not white).

 • Find someone who does not like bananas.

 • Find someone who had orange juice for breakfast.

 • Find someone who has a birthday in the same month as you.

© Instructional Fair • TS Denison   IF01366 Holidays for Dull Days

Graphing Similarities/Differences

	1	2	3	4	5	6	7
Blue Eyes							
Brown Eyes							
Green Eyes							
Boys							
Girls							
Colored Socks							
Dark Hair							
Light Hair							
Likes Dogs							
Likes Cats							

IF01366 Holidays for Dull Days

I like to play with balls.

I like to play outside.

I like dolls and soft things.

I like to sing and make music.

I like to color and paint.

I like to read books.

Day of Bread

Nutritional experts suggest we each eat six servings of breads and cereals daily.
Get your recommended daily allowance of bread by celebrating this fun holiday.

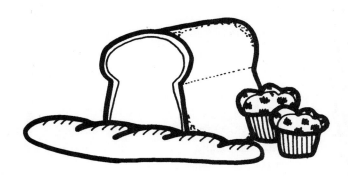

Day of Bread

Write "breakfast," "lunch," and "dinner" on three separate pieces of paper. Prepare the Day of Bread examples included at the end of this lesson as directed. Hold up each item and let the children decide whether the bread item you are displaying is typically a breakfast, lunch, or dinner bread. Are there some kinds of bread that are eaten at more than one meal?

Taste Test

Gather several different kinds of bread for the children to sample. Some kinds to consider are whole wheat, white, rye, cornbread, sourdough, and pumpernickel. Try to gather a variety of different forms of bread, also, such as tortillas, pitas, rolls, muffins, etc. Encourage the children to taste a small sample of every kind.

Bread Trails

Take several pieces of stale bread and tear them into 1" (25 mm) cubes. Let one child lay out a path of bread crumbs along the ground. Invite the other children to follow the trail left by the first child. Have the last child in line pick up the bread pieces and gather them back into a plastic bag. Repeat as time and interest allow.

Bread Animals

Thaw a package of frozen roll dough. Cover a clean table with a light dusting of flour.

Make sure the chilren have washed their hands thoroughly before molding their bread. Give each child two or three balls of dough to use in creating a bread animal by rolling, punching, and/or cutting the dough. Use raisins for eyes, if desired. Whip an egg white until fluffy and combine with 2 tbsp. (30 ml) water. Brush the completed creations with the egg mixture before baking as directed on the package. Keep track of which bread animal belongs to each child as you bake the bread creations, so that the bread animals can be eaten as a snack or taken home and shared with family members at the end of your Day of Bread.

Bread Shapes

Give each child a couple of slices of bread. Place the bread on a sheet of waxed paper, and then use cookie cutters to cut small shapes from the bread. Allow the children to eat the shapes they cut. Save the crusts in a plastic bag to feed the birds or to use for the Bread Trails activity.

Variation: Give each child a card with a number or math equation written on it. The child must then cut out the appropriate number of shapes to match the number or the sum of the equation before eating the snack.

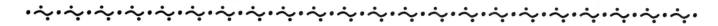

Build a Sandwich Game

Prepare the sandwich game by making a copy of the die (see page 103) on heavy cardstock. Color the pictures. Cut out the die pattern on the outside edges and then cut on the dotted lines. To make the die shape, fold on all solid lines and secure the edges of the shape by taping the tabs. Make one copy of the game pieces for each player. Color, cut them out, and laminate for durability.

To play, arrange one set of sandwich ingredient game pieces in the center of the playing area for each player. Have the first player roll the die. That child collects the game piece shown on the top of the die. Play continues with the next child rolling the die and receiving the corresponding sandwich piece. If the child rolls the die and already has the piece shown, the next child takes a turn by rolling the die. When "free choice" is shown on the die, the player may choose any piece he needs to add to his sandwich. The object of the game is to collect all five ingredients to make a sandwich. "Yum-yum!"

Making Homemade Bread

Follow the recipe shown to make your own loaves of bread. Be sure to discuss and observe the action of the yeast as the bread is being prepared.

Extension: Discuss what yeast is and what is does for bread. Make three different batches, observing the following differences in the dough as you change the yeast content. Make one loaf as directed. Make a second loaf without any yeast. Make a third loaf by doubling the yeast content. Be sure to record your predictions and discoveries.

If possible, investigate how temperature affects the yeast. Divide the dough in half and observe what happens when one dough is placed in a cool location (refrigerator) and the other dough is placed in a warm area to rise.

Wheat Bread

3½ c. (840 ml) warm water
1 pkg. yeast
1 tbsp. (15 ml) salt
½ c. (118 ml) sugar
½ c. (118 ml) shortening
3 c. (711 ml) whole wheat flour
white flour

Dissolve yeast in ½ c. (120 ml) of the warm water. Combine shortening, sugar, and salt in a mixing bowl. Add remaining water and mix. Blend in yeast. Add whole wheat flour and mix thoroughly. Add white flour until moderately stiff dough is formed. Knead for 10 minutes. Place the dough in a warm place and let it rise. Punch down, shape into two loaves, and place in bread pans. Let the dough rise again until it is rounded over the edge of the pan. Bake at 375° for 35 minutes.

Story Time

Read *Bread, Bread, Bread* by Ann Morris (Lothrop, Lee & Shepard, 1985). Use the information as a springboard to investigate other types of bread, including breads that are familiar to your students but are eaten in other cultures and countries.

Extension: Visit a bakery to observe how bread is made.

Day of Bread

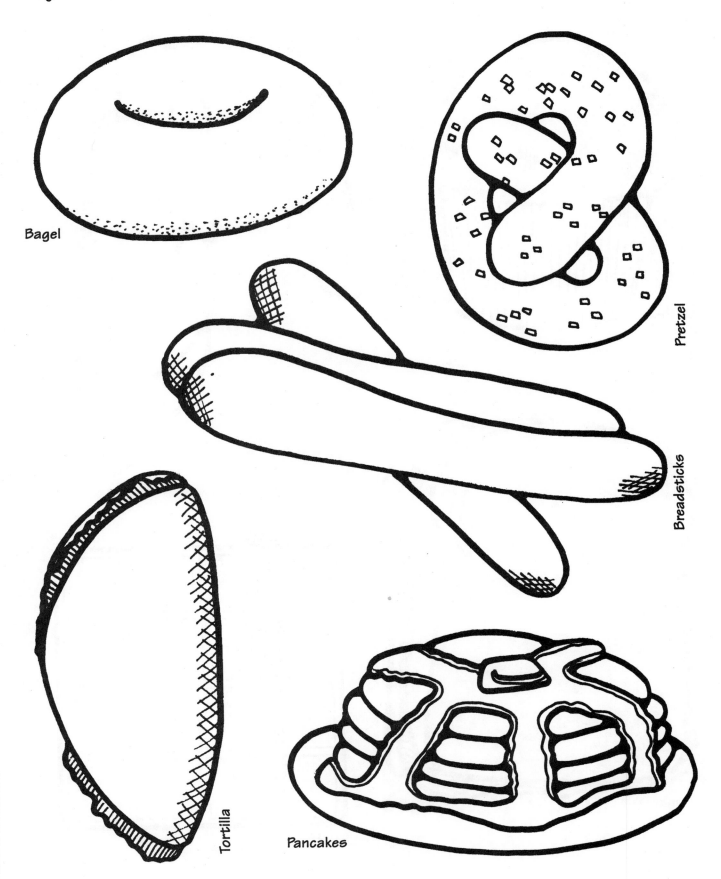

Bagel

Pretzel

Breadsticks

Tortilla

Pancakes

Muffins

Rolls

Sandwich

Waffle

102

Build a Sandwich Game Die

Fold and glue here.

Cut here.

Cut here.

Cut here.

Cut here.

Cut here.

Free!

Cut here.

Cut here.

IF01366 Holidays for Dull Days

Build a Sandwich Game Pieces

Peanut Butter Lover's Month

George Washington Carver came up with over 300 uses and inventions for peanuts—peanut butter is only one of them. Here is a day of celebration you can go pea-NUTS over! Note: Be sure to check for any food allergies students may have before attempting this unit.

Peanut Math

Use peanuts to measure the lengths of objects or the distances to locations around the classroom. If interested, measure the objects listed on the Noodle Measurement sheet on page 32, using "peanuts" instead of noodles. Record the measurements on a large chart.

Premeasure several bags of peanuts (fill the bags with small weight increments). Compare the masses of objects in the classroom with the bags of peanuts on a balance. Or, using a bathroom scale, have the children find out how many bags of peanuts it would take to equal their own weights.

Peanut Butter

Make your own peanut butter by blending 1 c. (237 ml) of roasted peanuts and 2 tbsp. (15 ml) oil on high in a blender until smooth and creamy. Add a pinch of salt to season and spread your work on crackers for others to taste.

Peanut Butter Sandwiches

Peanut butter sandwiches are arguably the most popular childhood sandwich. They are also simple for children to make. Place bread, peanut butter, jam or honey (optional), plastic knives, and paper towels on a table and let the children create their own snacks.

Peanut Butter Sandwich Sequencing

Use the Peanut Butter Sandwich Sequencing activity page to create sequencing cards. Photocopy, color as desired, and cut apart the cards. If desired, laminate them for durability. Have the children identify which picture comes first, second, third, and so on, creating a peanut butter sandwich.

Variation: You may wish to make a copy of this activity page for each child to color, cut out, and create a set of picture cards.

Sandwich Me Tag

In this variation of tag, two children are chosen to be "It." They must hold hands while trying to catch other children. Once a child is tagged by one or the other of the "It team," they must stand still while the "It team" sandwiches them in a hug.

P-nutty Bag Game

Gather three identical brown paper lunch bags and enough peanuts in their shells for the children. Place one peanut inside one of the bags. Fold the tops down so that the children cannot see inside. Set the bags in front of you and then mix them up by moving the bags and trading places. See if the children can keep track of which bag is holding the peanut. Choose a child to guess and check to see if he is correct. If so, give him the peanut from the bag. Replace the peanut, mix the bags up, and continue playing with another child.

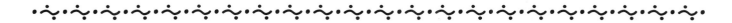

Peanut Butter Betty

Peanut Butter Betty is all butterfingers when it comes to making her own sandwich. Prepare for this activity by cutting 32 small circle or "blob" shapes out of brown construction paper or paper bags, make one or more sets depending how many children will be using them. Prepare Peanut Butter Betty by coloring and laminating the activity page provided at the end of this lesson—one for each pair of students or one for the large group.

Have the children help you tell the "Peanut Butter Betty" story provided at the end of this lesson by taking turns in placing a peanut butter "blob" on Betty's face every time the words "peanut butter" appear in the story. When the story is finished, use the blobs to count how many times "peanut butter" appeared in the story.

Extension: Talk about food preferences. Survey the class to see if they could eat only one thing exclusively for a day or a week.

For more information about peanuts, contact the American Peanut Council Education Service P.O. Box 845, Nashville, NC 27856-0845. Telephone number: (252) 459-9977. Fax: (252) 459-7396. Web site: www.aboutpeanuts.com or www.peanutsusa.com

Peanut Butter Play-Dough

Not only can you make wonderful creations with this play-dough, but when you are done playing with it, you may either eat your creation or keep the dough in the refrigerator for another day.

Play-Dough

1 c. (237 ml) peanut butter
1 c. (240 ml) light corn syrup
1 ¼ c. (295 ml) powdered milk
¼ c. (59 ml) powdered sugar

Mix all ingredients together. If the dough is too sticky, add a little powdered milk. Knead, roll, and shape as desired. Store in the refrigerator.

Peanut Shell Recycling

Peanut shells can be messy, but they can also be turned into fun learning tools and art supplies.

Peanut People: The unusual and unique shape of peanuts-in-the-shell are great to use in creating an assortment of people. Using markers, draw faces, hair, clothes, or other features onto the peanut shells. You may also wish to use small felt scraps to dress your peanut people. (You can also create your own zoo out of the odd-shaped peanut shells.) Use all the peanut people in one large scene or have the children draw background pictures (such as a beach or a birthday party) and then add the peanut people to complete the scenes.

Peanut Mosaics: Color the peanut shells by spray painting them in several different colors. Let the children use the shells to create pictures on paper or to trace lines or words.

Peanut Counters: Use the peanut shells (color if desired as instructed above) as tokens for working out math problems.

Peanut Hunt

Choose one child to leave the room. Have another child hide a peanut (in the shell) somewhere within view (such as on a bookshelf or on top of another child's head). Invite the first child to return to the room and look for the peanut. As the child is looking, you may wish to have the rest of the class assist by chanting "peanut butter, peanut butter" louder and louder as the child approaches the hiding place. Once the peanut is found, have the child who found the peanut choose the next child, and have the child who hid the peanut choose his/her replacement. Repeat as time and interest allow.

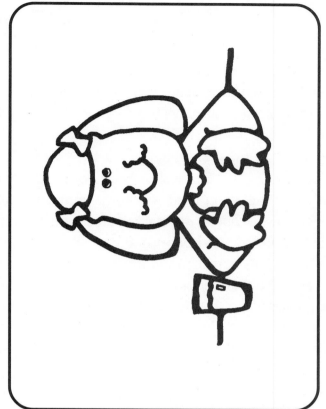

Peanut Butter Betty

Betty loved **peanut butter** sandwiches. She absolutely LOVED **peanut butter** sandwiches. In fact, Betty loved **peanut butter** sandwiches better than anything else in the whole world.

Betty's mother would often try to get Betty to eat things like broccoli, and chicken soup, but Betty always refused, insisting that she have **peanut butter** sandwiches instead. So Betty generally had **peanut butter** sandwiches for breakfast, and **peanut butter** sandwiches for lunch, and **peanut butter** sandwiches for dinner. She even had **peanut butter** sandwiches for snack time. Betty sometimes had dreams that she was eating **peanut butter** sandwiches in her sleep.

"You'd better be careful, or you'll turn into a **peanut butter** sandwich someday," warned Betty's mother. But Betty just rolled her eyes and took another bite of her **peanut butter** sandwich.

Finally Betty's mother could handle this **peanut butter** sandwich business no more. "If you want **peanut butter** sandwiches to eat, Betty," her mother said, "you'll have to make your own **peanut butter** sandwiches from now on. I am on a **peanut butter** sandwiches strike!" With that, Betty's mother put down her knife and left Betty with her **peanut butter** sandwiches in the kitchen all alone.

This was all fine and well with Betty. Now Betty could make **peanut butter** sandwiches all day long if she cared to. Betty picked up the knife, opened the jar of **peanut butter**, and scooped out enough **peanut butter** to make a **peanut butter** sandwich the size of Texas. She began to spread the **peanut butter** on the bread, but things quickly got out of hand. Before she knew it, the entire kitchen was covered in a thick gooey **peanut butter** mess.

Betty was covered head to toe with **peanut butter**. She had **peanut butter** in her hair, **peanut butter** in her ears, **peanut butter** in her eyelashes, **peanut butter** under her chin, and although she couldn't be quite sure of it, Betty thought she may have **peanut butter** up her nose. Betty began to cry. But instead of tears, thick gooey **peanut butter** came out of her eyes and plopped to the floor. Betty began to cry louder and louder until her mother finally came running to see what all the fuss was about. "I'll never eat another **peanut butter** sandwich as long as I live," wailed Betty.

Betty's mother began wiping the **peanut butter** from Betty's face and said, "At least not for the rest of the day, dear."

Betty gave her mother a big **peanut butter** hug and kiss.

Have a Bad Day Day

You have heard of having a bad hair day.
Here is a day to celebrate having an all-around bad day—just for the fun of it!

A Really Bad Day!

Obtain a copy of *Alexander and The Terrible, Horrible, No Good, Very Bad Day* by Judith Viorst (Aladdin Books, 1987) to read to the children. Invite the children to share their experiences with having a really bad day.

Extension: After reading the story, have the children write their own books, inserting their names into the titles. Be sure to encourage the children to write about experiences they encountered on a bad day, real or imagined, and include endings that allow them to resolve their bad days.

Grouch Collage

You may be having a bad day, but you are usually not the only one. Have several magazines (news magazines are best for this activity), scissors, paper, and paste on hand to make a grouch collage. Have the children search through the magazines for pictures of people who look like they are having a bad day. Cut the pictures out and paste them on a piece of plain paper.

Variation: Choose a photograph from a magazine depicting a person who appears to be having a bad day. Write a story about this person, imagining what may have happened to cause the bad day, and explaining how the person resolved his/her grouchy feelings.

Match My Face

Make a copy of the Match My Face activity page provided at the end of this lesson. Color as desired. Cut out the cards and place one card in each pocket of a multi-pocketed apron or jacket. Let a child choose a card from one of the pockets. Show the card to the children, discuss which emotion is being exemplified and have the children see if they can make the same expression on their faces. Repeat until all the pockets have been emptied. Place the cards on a table next to a mirror for the children to use when trying to make the faces on their own.

Extension: Divide the class into teams of two. Have one child draw a game card without showing it to the other player. When the child mimics the face on the card, the second child must then try to guess the emotion the first child is exhibiting.

Sneak Up on the Grouch Game

Choose one child to be "Grouch." Have Grouch turn her face to the wall and fold her arms. Line the rest of the class against the wall on the opposite side of the room. When Grouch stomps her foot, the class quietly begins sneaking up on Grouch, attempting to tag her before she hears them. Should Grouch hear someone in the class making noise while approaching her, she can growl, "Somebody's making me grumpy." Everyone must take three large steps backwards and wait for Grouch to begin the game again by stomping her foot. The new Grouch is the first child to tag Grouch without being heard.

Grouch Game

Duplicate the game board on pages 114–115. Color it as desired, laminate, and mount on tagboard. Make a copy of the Match My Face activity page, color, and separate the cards. Use small game markers for player pieces. Make a set of index cards with numbers or math equations written on them for the draw pile, or use a die to advance the players around the board. To play, draw from the deck of number cards (or roll the die). Move the number of spaces indicated on the card. If the space you land on is a happy face, tell of an experience that made you feel happy, and move ahead one space. Play resumes to the left. If the space you land on is a grumpy face, relate an experience that made you feel grumpy and what you did to feel happy again. You must then move back one space and play resumes to the next player. If the space you land on is a star, choose a card from the Match My Face Cards, identify the emotion being displayed on the card, and mimic the face. The first player to reach the last square on the path is declared the winner.

Variation: Since you are celebrating "Have a Bad Day Day," reverse the rules so that when you land on a happy face, you must move back a space. Move forward one space when you land on a grumpy face.

Grouch Mask

Make one copy of the Grouch Mask activity page provided at the end of this lesson for each child. Have the child color and cut out the face, being sure to draw a REALLY grouchy frown. Cut out the eye holes where indicated. Attach a craft stick or straw to the back with a piece of masking tape. Have the child hold up the mask when talking about grouchy feelings.

When I'm Happy/When I'm Sad

Prepare a happy/sad stick for each child by cutting out a circle, approximately 3" (76 mm) in diameter. Draw a simple happy face on one side, and a sad/frowning face on the other. Attach the circle to a craft stick or straw with masking tape.

Sing "When You're Happy and You Know It" as a group. Next, decide as a group what you would do if you were sad, grumpy, or otherwise having a bad day. Sing the song again replacing the words, "When you're sad (grumpy) and you know it _____." Talk about how your feelings are different when you are sad or grumpy than when you are happy. Have the children show you what a sad face and a happy face look like with their own faces.

Give each child a happy/sad stick. Let the children show you which side is "happy" and which side is "sad." Present the children with the following scenarios (or you may come up with your own) and have them show you if that situation would make them happy (by showing the happy face on the stick) or sad (by showing the sad face):

"How do you feel when . . .
- you drop your ice cream cone?
- your parent tells you it's time for bed?
- you learn to ride a bike?
- you skin your knee?
- you work hard to color a picture?
- your pet dies?
- you get to choose where the family will eat for dinner?
- you get to stay up past your bedtime?
- your friend says she/he won't play with you?

I Am Grouchy When . . .

Write the title "I Am Grouchy When . . ." on drawing paper for each child. Have the child draw a picture of herself in a situation where she is grouchy. Invite the child to tell about her picture as you record the words on the paper. Be sure to read the ideas back to the child when you have finished.

Cut out.

IF01366 Holidays for Dull Days

Grouch Game

Bathtub Party Day

Most children bathe regularly to clean and deodorize their skin.
Celebrate Bathtub Party Day for some good clean fun!

Rubber Ducky Race

Fill a small wading pool or water table with water. Obtain two or three rubber ducks, or fill yellow water balloons one-third full of water and inflate. Tie a knot to keep each balloon from loosing air, and then draw eyes above the knots to create your own ducks.

Let the children each choose a duck and place it in the "tub." Now use any means (splashing, making waves, etc.) to get each duck from one end of the tub to the other without touching it. Repeat so that all the children have an opportunity to race a duck.

Extension: Prepare more ducks for the activity. Write numbers on the bottoms of half of the rubber ducks, then write the corresponding dots or math equations on the bottoms of the second set of ducks. The children must then try to find the matching ducks.

Bubble Color Pop

Prepare three separate bowls of bubble solution by coloring the bubble solution red, yellow and blue with liquid food coloring. Place a sheet of paper in the bottom of a 9" x 13" (23 x 33 cm) pan. Dip a bubble wand in one of the colored bowls, lean directly over the paper and blow. The bubbles float onto the paper and pop leaving a beautifully colored bubble impression.

Water Explorations

Sink/Float: Find different objects around the classroom and predict whether they will sink or float once they are placed in the water. Have the children test their predictions, and see if they can theorize why each item did or did not sink.

Boat Float: Provide several different materials, such as Styrofoam trays, paper plates, clay, and wood scraps. Have the children try to create boats that float with various materials. Can the materials be manipulated so that the boats will float? (For example, a ball of clay will not float, but if it is flattened and shaped into a cup, it will float.) How many paper clips can you stack on your boat before it sinks?

Investigating Surface Tension: Fill a small plastic glass with water as close to the rim as possible without letting the water spill over the edge. Slowly add paper clips to the glass—one at a time. Watch what happens to the surface of the water. (You will see a "dome" of water that extends over the top of the glass.) Find out how many paper clips can be added before the surface tension is broken and the water spills over the edge of the cup.

Variation: Experiment with pennies, marbles, or other small objects. Does the size or weight of the objects affect your experiment?

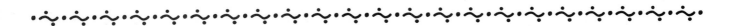

Making Soap

You can make your own soap by mixing soap flakes with a little bit of water. Start with 1 cup (237 ml) soap flakes and add water 1 tbsp. (15 ml) at a time until the mixture is a sticky consistency but can be molded. Press into cookie cutters to make shapes. Let your soap dry before using it to lather up in the tub!

Me in the Tub

Make a copy of page 122 for each child. Have the child draw a picture of her/himself in the tub with a favorite bathtub toy. Do not forget to add the bubbles!

Variations: Use the Me in the Tub activity page as the cover to a booklet. Have the children write stories about themselves and other objects being inside a tub full of bubbles.

Make an alphabet booklet where the child writes each letter of the alphabet on a page and then draws or finds a magazine picture to match the letter of an object that can be added to the tub. At the end of the story the child has MANY things in the tub full of bubbles.

Soap Finger Paint

Mix powdered laundry detergent and enough water to create a thick soapy mixture. Whip the mixture until all the detergent has been dissolved and the soap is foamy. Add a few drops of food coloring to tint the soap, then mix thoroughly.

Spread the soap bubbles on a sheet of waxed paper or finger-painting paper. Let the children finger paint designs in the soap.

Bathtub Races

Gather two boxes; each large enough so that a child can sit comfortably inside. Punch two holes on either side of the box, about 4" (102 mm) from the end of the box and 2" (51 mm) from the top. Thread a length of rope through the holes and knot securely. Let two teams of three children each (one to push, one to pull, and one to ride inside the box) race against another team around a designated course in the room.

Inside a Tub Full of Bubbles

Prepare the Inside a Tub Full of Bubbles illustrations provided on pattern pages 119–121. Copy the pictures on heavy cardstock, then color them as desired and cut them out. Attach felt or flannel to the back of the illustrations. While showing the pictures tell the story on page 118. Be sure to add each character to the tub as it is mentioned in the story.

Extension: Write each of the lines of the last paragraph of the story on separate sentence strips. Have the children retell the story by ordering the sentence strips. If appropriate, use the word strips to look for rhyming words, match beginning sounds, or for other phonemic awareness activities.

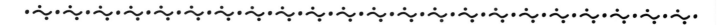

Inside a Tub Full of Bubbles

Here is a tub full of bubbles.
Here is a boy that is ready to scrub
Inside a tub full of bubbles.

Here is a boy that is ready to scrub
And can't find the soap, (it's lost in the tub),
Inside a tub full of bubbles.

Here is a boy that is ready to scrub
And can't find the soap, (it's lost in the tub),
Underneath a moose who has suds on his nose,
Inside a tub full of bubbles.

Here is a boy that is ready to scrub
And can't find the soap, (it's lost in the tub),
Underneath a moose who has suds on his nose,
Next to a snake who is sniffing a rose,
Inside a tub full of bubbles.

Here is a boy that is ready to scrub
And can't find the soap, (it's lost in the tub),
Underneath a moose who has suds on his nose,
Next to a snake who is sniffing a rose,
That's making the kangaroo sniffle and sneeze,
Inside a tub full of bubbles.

Here is a boy that is ready to scrub
And can't find the soap, (it's lost in the tub),
Underneath a moose who has suds on his nose,
Next to a snake who is sniffing a rose,
That's making the kangaroo sniffle and sneeze,
Big soapy bubbles on the brown camel's knees
Inside a tub full of bubbles.

Here is a boy that is ready to scrub
And can't find the soap, (it's lost in the tub),
Underneath a moose who has suds on his nose,
Next to a snake who is sniffing a rose,
That's making the kangaroo sniffle and sneeze,
Big soapy bubbles on the brown camel's knees,
Which are causing the shark to wiggle and jump,
Inside a tub full of bubbles.

Here is a boy that is ready to scrub
And can't find the soap, (it's lost in the tub),
Underneath a moose who has suds on his nose,
Next to a snake who is sniffing a rose,
That's making the kangaroo sniffle and sneeze,
Big soapy bubbles on the brown camel's knees,
Which are causing the shark to wiggle and jump,
Poking the rhino right in the rump,
Inside a tub full of bubbles.

Yes, there's sneezing and poking and chaos galore
Inside a tub full of bubbles.

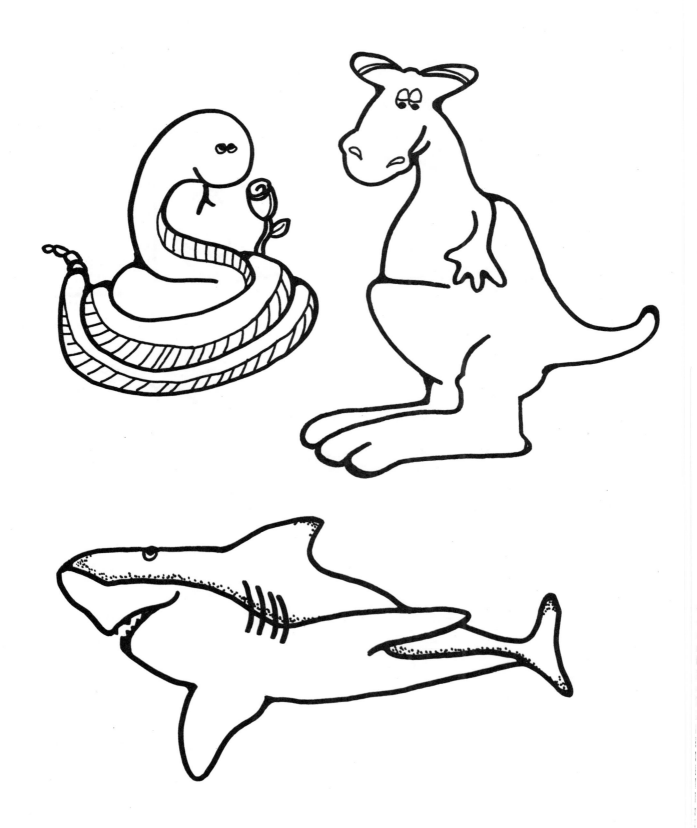

Me in the Tub . . .

IF01366 *Holidays for Dull Days*

Wright Brothers' Day

On December 17, 1903, Orville and Wilber Wright manned the first recorded air flight at Kitty Hawk, North Carolina. Use these activities to take off on your own fun.

Exploration Activity

Locate books on airplanes and other aircraft. Discuss the similarities and differences of various aircrafts and their purposes. Locate a picture of the evolution of the airplane—particularly the type that Orville and Wilber Wright would have flown. Compare it to modern airplanes.

Excursion

If you live in an area that is close to an airport, make an appointment to tour the airport as a group, or go to a grassy place where you can watch the airplanes land and take off as you have a picnic lunch.

Air or Land?

Gather several items (or pictures of things) that you generally find in the air, such as clouds, birds, airplanes, and hot air balloons. Gather another set of things you typically find on land, like people, cars, and trees. Place each item in a brown paper bag and fold down the top so that the contents cannot be seen. Set up a divider (such as a blanket stretched between two chairs) so that a child sitting behind the divider cannot seen by the other children.

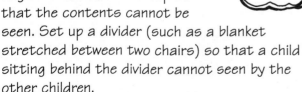

Choose one child to come up and select a bag. Have the child walk behind the divider, remove the contents of the bag, and describe it to the other children without actually telling what it is. Once the children have guessed the object, decide if it is something that you would find in the air or on land. Continue until all the objects have been described.

Airplane Races

Fold several simple airplanes as shown on page 128. Place a piece of tape along the floor to designate the starting point. Draw an "x" on a large piece of paper and tape it to the floor approximately 8 ft. (2.44 m) away. Let the children stand at the line and experiment with their airplanes to see if they can fly them and land them on the "x."

Variation: Try altering your paper airplane by folding, bending, or cutting the airplane's wings or nose to see how it affects the airplane's performance. Try making different sizes or styles of airplanes to see which one flies the best, the farthest, and so on. Measure the distance each airplane travels.

Wind Experiments

Airplanes use the physical property called the Bernoulli Effect in order to fly. Simply put, this means that there is more air pressure under the airplane wing than there is over the wing, causing the wing to be "pushed up" into the air. Situate a large box fan face up between two chairs so that it is secure, but so that the fan can draw air from between the chairs. Take a large, lightweight ball such as a beach ball or balloon and place it directly over the fan. What happens to the ball? Experiment with other objects such as a piece of paper or a heavier ball. Discuss which items will fly, telling why or why not.

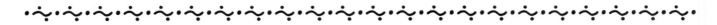

Postcards from the Trip

Make a copy of the postcard pattern for each child to create a postcard for a favorite imaginary vacation spot. Be sure to have the children add their addresses where indicated on the right side of the cards and create their own stamps. On the left side of the cards, have the children write about their experiences on their imaginary travels. Encourage the children to include things they have done or seen while "vacationing." On the backs of the postcards, have the children draw pictures of their vacation destinations.

Things in the Sky

Make a copy for each child of the Things in the Sky pattern pages provided at the end of this lesson. Have each child color the pages as desired and cut out the objects. Punch three holes (indicated by small dots) on the bottom of the large cloud. Punch a hole at the top of each figure where indicated by a small dot. Cut four lengths of string or yarn and tie the airplane, helicopter, and cloud to the large cloud. Punch another hole at the small dot at the top of the large cloud and tie with a string. Hang the mobile from the ceiling.

Variation: Have the children list as many things (e.g., birds, zeppelins, rain, hot air balloons, airplanes) as possible that are found in the sky on the mobile cloud.

Up, Up, and Away

Set up two rows of chairs (place the chairs one in front of the other) with an aisle down the middle. Number the chairs by taping a small numbered scrap of paper to the seat of each chair. Tell the children that today they are going for an airplane ride. Give each child a scrap of paper with his/her name written on it and a number that corresponds to a seat number on the airplane. Remind the children that they must use their tickets to get on the plane.

Begin calling the children to the plane and invite them to find their correct seats by matching the numbers on their tickets to the numbers on the chairs. Once the child has successfully found his seat, remind him that it is very important to be safe while riding an airplane, so he must always stay seated.

As the airplane "takes off," have the children slowly lean back into their seats until the plane reaches the correct altitude and levels off. Invite the children to look out their "windows" to see interesting things on the ground. Have the children use their imaginations to tell you what they see. After everyone has had an opportunity to describe what they can see out their "windows," tell them you will be coming through the cabin with snacks and beverages. Serve small cups of crackers or pretzels with small glasses of juice or water. Be sure to pick up all the empty cups before landing. As the children leave the flight, invite them to fly with you again sometime.

Variation: Place a large map of your state, province, or country, or a world map on a wall nearby your airplane setup. Mark a few prominent cities, landmarks, or destinations on the map and mark a travel path from your city to these destinations by stretching a piece of string or by drawing a colored line between the two locations. On a chart, list the destinations, the distances in miles or kilometers between the destinations, and a ticket price for each location. Provide paper money for the children to use—giving each child a predetermined sum.

Before getting on the flight, the children must determine a destination (e.g., "I want to travel to Disney World"). Each child must figure out how much money it would take to purchase a ticket, or if the child wants to travel to more than one distination, she must determine if she has enough money to purchase both tickets. (Make a copy of the Trip Planner on page 127 for each child to use.)

Other activities may include adding the miles for trips to more than one destination.

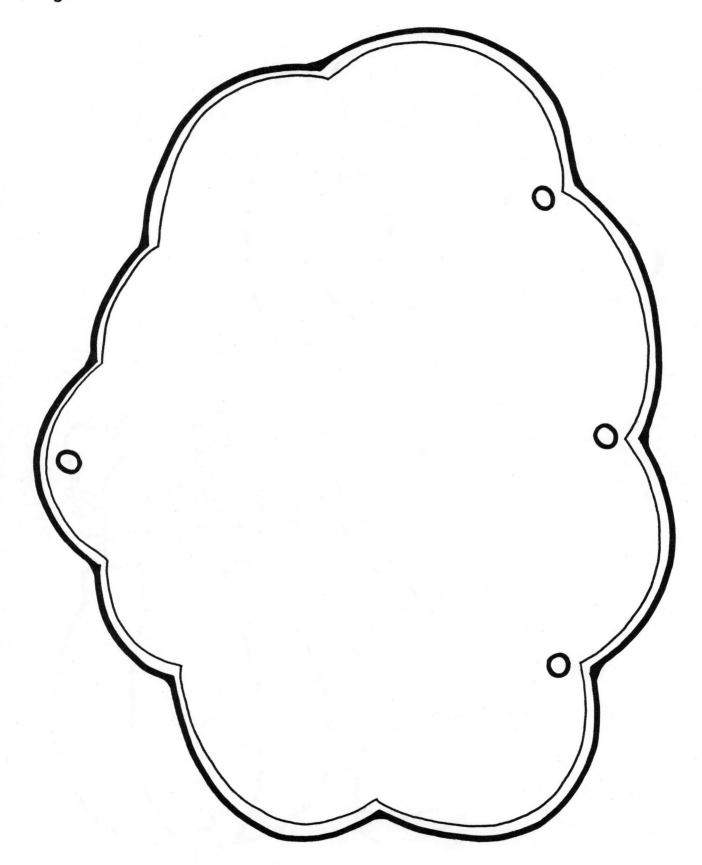

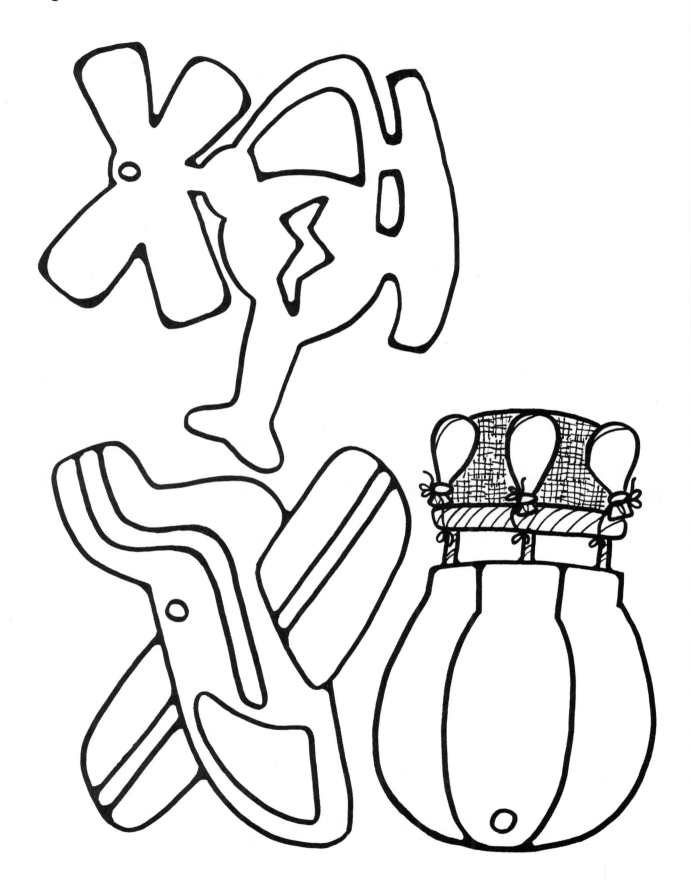

I would like to fly to

The ticket costs $\$$ _____.

IF01366 Holidays for Dull Days

Making Paper Airplanes

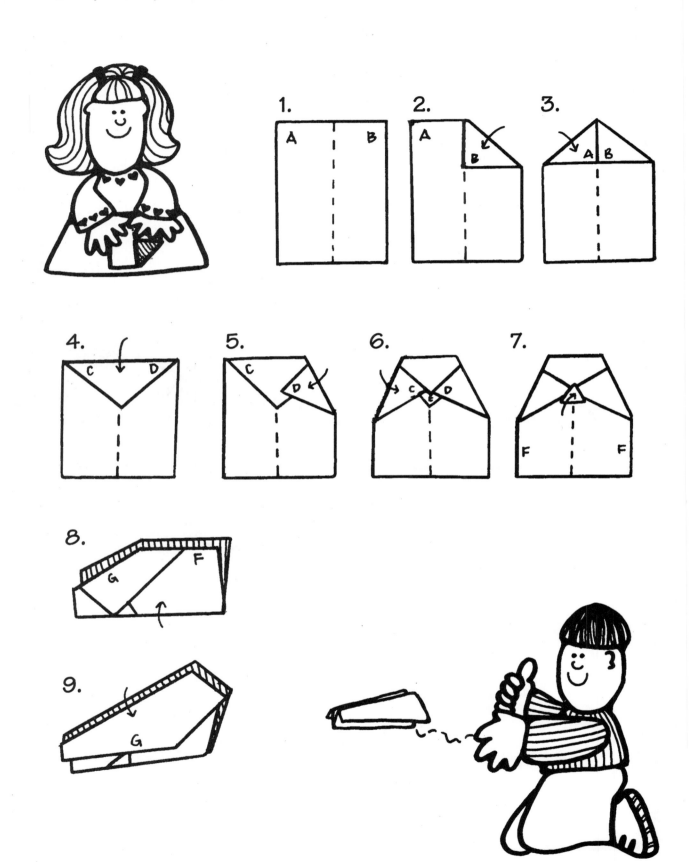

128